STUDY GUIDE

for

Larry J. Siegel's

CRIMINOLOGY

Sixth Edition

Alex Alvarez
Northern Arizona University

West/Wadsworth
I(T)P® An International Thomson Publishing Company

Belmont, CA • Albany, NY • Bonn • Boston • Cincinnati • Detroit • Johannesburg • London
Madrid • Melbourne • Mexico City • New York • Paris • Singapore • Tokyo • Toronto • Washington

Printed in the United States of America
1 2 3 4 5 6 7 8 9 10

For more information, contact Wadsworth Publishing Company, 10 Davis Drive, Belmont, CA 94002, or electronically at http://www.thomson.com/wadsworth.html

International Thomson Publishing Europe
Berkshire House 168-173
High Holborn
London, WC1V 7AA, England

Thomas Nelson Australia
102 Dodds Street
South Melbourne 3205
Victoria, Australia

Nelson Canada
1120 Birchmount Road
Scarborough, Ontario
Canada M1K 5G4

International Thomson Publishing GmbH
Königswinterer Strasse 418
53227 Bonn, Germany

International Thomson Editores
Campos Eliseos 385, Piso 7
Col. Polanco
11560 México D.F. México

International Thomson Publishing Asia
221 Henderson Road
#05-10 Henderson Building
Singapore 0315

International Thomson Publishing Japan
Hirakawacho Kyowa Building, 3F
2-2-1 Hirakawacho
Chiyoda-ku, Tokyo 102, Japan

International Thomson Publishing Southern Africa
Building 18, Constantia Park
240 Old Pretoria Road
Halfway House, 1685 South Africa

ISBN 0-534-53525-9

Contents

Student Introduction

How do people learn anything? For many, learning a complicated subject requires a plan of action. We need a method to help us grasp and hold on to difficult concepts and theories. Educators know that the more you think and write about what you've learned, the greater the probability that you'll understand and retain the material. This study guide offers a means for you to be a more active learner by becoming more engaged in the learning process.

Keep in mind that this book is intended as a supplementary aid to the book, and is not intended to replace the text. Rather it has been designed to assist and enhance your comprehension of the major concepts, theories, and issues related to the field of criminology. Specifically, the guide has been structured to provide you with valuable tools for mastering the content presented in the sixth edition of <u>Criminology</u> written by Larry J. Siegel, an unequaled introductory text to the field.

The guide's structure is simple and straight forward. Each chapter is broken into nine sections.

- **LEARNING OBJECTIVES** that should orient you to the content and help you broadly conceptualize the learning expectations for the chapter.

- **KEY TERMS AND CONCEPTS** that are intended to sensitize you to the specialized vocabulary in the chapter.

- **NAMES TO KNOW** that will assist in familiarizing you with the important personalities and criminologists reviewed in the chapter.

The following sections offer a variety of test questions designed to assist you in learning the material and preparing for in class tests. While the questions are not exhaustive, they are representative of the material covered in each chapter and should provide a comprehensive tool to facilitate understanding of the chapter content. The last section provides the correct answers so that you can check your performance.

- **FILL-IN REVIEW**.

- **TRUE/FALSE**

- **MULTIPLE CHOICE**

- **MATCHING**

- **ESSAY QUESTIONS**

- **ANSWER SECTION**

Below please find a brief series of recommendations about how this workbook can best be used in both internalizing the materials in the text and preparing you for examinations:

1. Use the text and study guide together.
2. Skim through the text to get an idea of what you will be reading.
3. Survey the chapter to be studied. Briefly examine the important sections and themes that are covered.
4. Turn to the study guide and read the LEARNING OBJECTIVES to familiarize yourself with the key issues that will be examined in the chapter.
5. Review the KEY TERMS AND CONCEPTS to help you in identifying significant points as they appear in the chapter. They are listed in the order in which they appear in the text. (As a review exercise, you may later want to write brief explanations or definitions of the key terms, etc.)
6. Review the NAMES TO KNOW to help you in identifying significant theorists, personalities, and criminologists as they appear in the chapter. They are usually listed in the order in which they appear in the text, although if an individuals name appears several times in a chapter they are only listed once. (As a review exercise, you may later want to briefly describe the significance of their work)
7. Carefully read the chapter itself. Highlight and outline as you review the chapter paying special attention to the terms, concepts, and people covered in the study guide.
8. Before taking the SELF TEST, you should review the aims of the LEARNING OBJECTIVES, and think about the meanings of the KEY TERMS AND CONCEPTS, and NAMES TO KNOW. This should help prepare you for taking the self test for the first time.
9. Take the SELF TEST as if it were the actual exam. This section contains FILL-IN REVIEW TRUE/FALSE, MULTIPLE CHOICE, MATCHING, AND ESSAY QUESTIONS.
   a. Most of the material in this section has also been presented in sequential order with the text narrative. Some items, however, are not arranged in sequence. These items represent a slightly greater degree of difficulty.
   b. Often you will discover that each question item tests a different concept, problem, or issue. Therefore, it may be prudent for you to try to answer every question.
   c. Please note that the questions vary in complexity. Questions have been designed along a difficulty continuum so it will be natural to find some questions harder than others.
10. Turn to the ANSWER SECTION at the back of the chapter to evaluate your accuracy in completing the self test.
   a. The text should be reviewed until all the correct answers can be identified and understood.
   b. Many of the items to be completed have been sequentially arranged with text material. Hopefully, this ordering will help you locate the correct responses in the text. Nevertheless, some items are not arranged in sequence and represent a further challenge to you.
   c. Have patience if you do not do as well as you would like. Good results may require your studying the material several times and testing yourself each time. Reread and rethink the textbook and review the study guide until you feel confident with the ideas. Be aware of your own attention span. Take time off between study sessions to refresh and reward yourself. Spaced or distributed learning is more productive than intensive, one shot learning.

The study of criminal behavior is both fascinating and exciting. We hope that your introductory experience to this field meets your expectations. Good luck and enjoy your exploration!

1 *Crime and Criminology*

LEARNING OBJECTIVES

1. Define criminology as an interdisciplinary and scientific discipline.

2. Contrast the crime problem in the United States with other societies.

3. Compare the field of criminology to criminal justice.

4. Examine the similarities and differences between crime and deviance.

5. Highlight important benchmarks in the history of criminology.

6. Trace the development of sociological criminology.

7. Understand the range of criminological investigation.

8. Compare and contrast the consensus, conflict, and interactionist view of crime.

9. List and discuss the different types of research methods used by criminologists.

10. Explain why ethical issues in criminology are so important

KEY TERMS AND CONCEPTS

Intimate violence	Anomie	Consensus
Criminology	Sociological criminology	Interactionist
Verified principles	Chicago school	Moral Entrepeneurs
Interdisciplinary	Conflict criminology	Survey research
Criminal Justice System	Bourgeoisie	Cross-sectional research
Deviant behavior	Proletariat	Sampling
Legalized	Criminological enterprise	Populations
Decriminalized	Sociology of law	Cohort
Classical criminology	Theory Construction	Aggregate data
Free will	Criminal behavior systems	Experimental research
Positivism	White-collar crime	Observational research
Positivist criminology	Penology	Interview research
Criminal anthropology	Victiminology	Ethical issues
Atavistic anomalies		

2

NAMES TO KNOW

David Graham
Diane Zamora
Adrienne Jones
Edwin Sutherland and Donald Cressey
Harry Anslinger
Cesare Beccaria
Auguste Comte
Charles Darwin
J.K. Lavater
Franz Joseph Gall
Johann K. Spurzheim
Phillipe Pinel
Benjamin Rush
Henry Maudsley
Cesare Lombroso
Adolphe Quetelet
Emile Durkheim

Robert Ezra Park
Ernest W. Burgess
Louis Wirth
Karl Marx
Ralf Dahrendorf
George Vold
Willem Bonger
Marvin Wolfgang and Franco Ferracuti
Jack Kevorkian
Hans von Hentig
Stephen Schafer
George Herbert Meade
Charles Horton Cooley
W. I. Thomas
Claire Sterk-Elifson
William Whyte
Richard Herrnstein and Charles Murray

FILL-IN REVIEW

1. The percentage of the population sent to prison and jail in the United States exceeds that of such notoriously punitive countries as the Soviet Union and _____ _____.

2. _____ is the scientific approach to the study of criminal behavior.

3. While for most of the twentieth century, criminology's primary orientation has been _____, today it can be viewed as an integrated approach to the study of crime and criminals, influenced by the contributions from various disciplines

4. The _____ tradition developed as the scientific method began to take hold in Europe. This movement was inspired by new discoveries in biology, astronomy, and chemistry.

5. _____ behavior is behavior that departs from social norms.

6. The study of criminal _____ is one of the most crucial aspects of the criminological enterprise because without valid and reliable data sources, efforts to conduct research on crime and create criminological theories would be futile.

7. The study of _____ involves the correction and control of known criminal offenders.

8. Lombroso believed that criminals suffer from _____ anomalies--physically, they are throwbacks to more primitive times when people were savages.

9. Quetelet was a Belgian mathematician who began what is known as the _____ school of criminology.

10. According to the _____ view, the definition of crime is controlled by wealth, power, and position and not by moral consensus or the fear of social disruption.

11. The _____ view of crime is similar to the _____ perspective because they both suggest that behavior is outlawed when it offends people who maintain the social, economic, and political power necessary to have the law conform to their interests or needs.

12. Most surveys involve _____--selecting for study a limited number of subjects who are representative of entire groups sharing similar characteristics, called _____.

13. _____ surveys ask participants to describe in detail their recent and lifetime criminal activity.

14. _____ research involves the observation of a group of people who share a like characteristic (cohort) over time.

15. The _____ is an annual report that reflects the number of crimes reported by citizens to local police departments and the number of arrests made by police agencies in a given year.

16. To conduct _____ research, criminologists manipulate or intervene in the lives of their subjects in order to see the outcome or effect the intervention has.

17. A common criminological method is the first-hand _____ of criminals in order to gain insight into their motives and activities.

18. A critical issue facing students of criminology involves recognizing the field's political and social consequences. All too often, criminologists forget the social _____ they bear as experts in the area of crime and justice.

19. Crime, argued _____, can also be useful, and on occasion even healthy, for a society to experience.

TRUE/FALSE

1. The United States punishes both violent and property crimes more strictly than Germany.

2. Lombroso believed that serious offenders inherited criminal traits.

3. The rape rate in the United States is 26 times higher than that of Japan.

4. The objective of criminology, according to Sutherland and Cressey, is the development of a body of specific rules of procedure which would result in the equal application of treatment techniques to criminals.

5. All crimes are deviant.

6. According to the consensus view, crimes are behaviors believed to be repugnant to all elements of society.

7.   The consensus model of crime is probably accepted by a majority of practicing criminologists and is the one most often used in criminology texts.

8   Nearly 10,000 people were prosecuted throughout Europe for witchcraft during the sixteenth and seventeenth centuries.

9   One principle of the positivism school is that human behavior is a function of external forces that are within an individual's control.

10. The consensus view of crime would include violations of human dignity.

11. The interactionist perspective attributes economic and political motives to the process of defining crime.

12. From the interactionist perspective, laws against pornography and drugs are believed to be motivated more by moral crusades than by capitalist sensibilities.

13. To those who subscribe to the consensus view, crime has no meaning unless people react to it.

14. Surveys include interviewing or questioning a group of subjects about research topics under consideration.

15. Cross-sectional research is among the most widely used methods of criminological study.

16. Aggregate data can be used to focus on the macro psychological forces which affect crime.

17. A quasi-experiment is undertaken when it is impossible to randomly select subjects or manipulate conditions.

18. Criminological experiments are common because they are relatively easy and cost effective to conduct.

19. To obtain data, criminologists often mislead people as to the true purpose of their efforts.

MULTIPLE CHOICE

1.   The positivist tradition contends that:
     a.   human nature is a function of internal forces
     b.   problems are solved through the use of the scientific method
     c.   human behavior is within the control of individuals
     d.   none of the above ("a" thru "c")

2.   According to a report of the Sentencing Project, a private non-profit agency devoted to improving the justice system, the United States led the world with its _____ rate.
     a.   arson
     b.   prostitution
     c.   embezzlement
     d.   murder

3.   Authorities in Vietnam report a troubling increase in:
   a.   white collar crime
   b.   political crime
   c.   predatory crime
   d.   corporate crime
   e.   gang crime

4.   The _____ school sociologists and their contemporaries focused on the functions of social institutions and how their breakdown influences behavior.
   a.   New York
   b.   West Coast
   c.   French
   d.   British
   e.   Chicago

5.   Criminal justice scholars are primarily interested in:
   a.   examining and describing the etiology of crime
   b.   explaining and analyzing the nature of crime in society
   c.   describing the behavior of agencies of justice
   d.   none of the above ("a" thru "c")

6.   The sale and possession of marijuana was legal in this country until _____, when it became illegal under federal law.
   a.   1837
   b.   1857
   c.   1937
   d.   1957

7.   Which of the following is an example of a new version of a traditional or common act that Michigan has passed legislation to make a felony:
   a.   computer fraud
   b.   assisted suicide
   c.   airplane hijacking
   d.   illegally tapping into TV cable lines

8.   In The Division of Labor in Society, Durkheim described the consequences of the shift from a small, rural society which he labeled mechanical, to the more modern _____ society with a large urban population, division of labor and personal isolation.
   a.   "organic"
   b.   "anomic"
   c.   industrial
   d.   none of the above ("a" thru "c")

9.   The various schools of criminology developed over a period of _____ years.
   a.   50
   b.   100
   c.   200
   d.   300
   e.   400

6

10. In one famous 1937 article, Anslinger told how "an entire family was murdered by a youthful addict in Florida ... [who] with an axe had killed his father, mother, two brothers, and a sister." The young person was addicted to:
    a. marijuana
    b. heroin
    c. cocaine
    d. LSD

11. Oppressive labor conditions prevalent during the rise of industrial capitalism convinced _____ that the character of every civilization is determined by its mode of production--the way its people develop and produce material goods (materialism).
    a. Kevorkian
    b. Cooley
    c. Marx
    d. Whyte

12. Edwin Sutherland's analysis of business-related offenses helped coin the phrase _____ collar crime to describe economic crime activities.
    a. white
    b. gray
    c. blue
    d. khaki

13. This definition of crime asserts that certain people hold social power in a particular legal jurisdiction and use their influence to impose their definition of right and wrong on the rest of the population.
    a. conflict view
    b. interactionist view
    c. disintegration view
    d. nihilistic view

14. This view of crime suggests that society should intervene as little as possible in the lives of law violators lest they be labeled and stigmatized.
    a. consensus
    b. conflict
    c. interactionist
    d. none of the above

15. The _____ view of crime dominated criminological thought until the late 1960s.
    a. consensus
    b. conflict
    c. interactionist
    d. nihilistic
    e. disintegration

16. Surveys are:
    a. powerful because subjects are typically honest and forthright
    b. useful because it is relatively easy to guard against people who deliberately lie
    c. limited if the study involves the way people interact with one another
    d. none of the above are true about surveys

17. An approach in which one takes an intact group of known offenders and looks back into their early life experiences is:
    a. regressive analysis
    b. linear reactive design
    c. historical pattern analysis
    d. retrospective longitudinal study
    e. none of the above

18. An example of a time-series design:
    a. going into the field and participating in group activities
    b. bringing subjects into a structured laboratory setting and observing how they react to a predetermined condition or stimulus
    c. an examination of the lifestyle of a single group of people
    d. none of the above ("a" thru "c")

19. Major ethical issues in criminology include:
    a. Who is to be studied?
    b. How should studies be conducted?
    c. How much will it cost?
    d. both "a" and "b" are ethical issues
    e. all of the above are ethical issues ("a" thru "c")

20. English Physician Henry Maudsley believed that criminality was linked with:
    a. insanity
    b. sin
    c. education
    d. skull shape
    e. laziness

MATCHING

____	1. Research questions	A.	Stigma
____	2. Etiology	B.	Marvin Wolfgang
____	3. Marijuana use	C.	Hypotheses
____	4. Psychocriminologists	D.	Genetics
____	5. <u>Patterns in Crimina Homicide</u>	E.	Harry Anslinger
____	6. Biocriminologists	F.	Origin
____	7. Founder of sociology	G.	Substantive criminal law
____	8. External cranial characteristics	H.	Phrenologists
____	9. Consensus view	I.	Auguste Comte
____	10. Conflict view	J.	Political concept
____	11. Interactionist view	K.	Cognition
____	12. Cross-sectional research	L.	Subjects come from different backgrounds and groups

ESSAY QUESTIONS

1.   Identify and describe possible issues that are raised by the murder of Adrienne Jones.

2.   Compare the crime problem in the U.S. to other similarly situated countries.

3.   Describe criminology as an integrated approach to the study of criminal behavior.

4.   Compare deviant behavior to criminal behavior.

5.   Describe the views of Beccaria on the purposes of punishment.

6.   What were the views of Emile Durkheim toward crime?

7.   Compare the conflict view of crime to the interactionist perspective.

8.   Identify the various definitions of the concept of crime.

9.   Describe two research techniques used by criminologists to measure the nature and extent of criminal behavior.

10.   What problems exist in using research money from outside sources?

11.   What do criminologists do?

12.   List several questions that have "tormented" criminologists.

13.   How do professional criminologists view crime?

14.   Identify the various definitions of the concept of crime.

15.   Describe two major ethical issues in criminology.

CHAPTER ONE ANSWER SECTION

FILL-IN REVIEW

1.	South Africa	11.	interactionist, conflict
2.	Criminology	12.	sampling, populations
3.	sociological	13.	Self-report
4.	positivist	14.	Longitudinal
5.	Deviant	15.	Uniform Crime Report (UCR)
6.	statistics	16.	experimental
7.	penology	17.	observation
8.	atavistic	18.	responsibility
9.	cartographic	19.	Durkheim
10.	conflict		

TRUE/FALSE

1.	F	11.	F
2.	T	12.	T
3.	T	13.	F
4.	F	14.	T
5.	F	15.	T
6.	T	16.	F
7.	T	17.	T
8.	F	18.	F
9.	F	19.	T
10.	F		

MULTIPLE CHOICE

1.	b	11.	c
2.	d	12.	a
3.	c	13.	b
4.	e	14.	c
5.	c	15.	a
6.	c	16.	c
7.	b	17.	d
8.	a	18.	d
9.	c	19.	d
10.	a	20.	a

MATCHING

1.	C
2.	F
3.	E
4.	K
5.	B
6.	D
7.	I
8.	H
9.	G
10.	J
11.	A
12.	L

2 The Criminal Law and Its Processes

LEARNING OBJECTIVES

1. Describe the legal system in England prior to and after the Norman Conquest in 1066, highlighting important changes.

2. Explain the origins and early development of the common law

3. Identify and describe the different ways that law can be classified.

4. Describe the different functions of criminal law.

5. Discuss the legal definition of a crime.

6. Identify and differentiate between the different types of intent.

7. Describe the differences between excuse and justification as types of defenses.

8. Differentiate between the different legal tests of insanity.

9. Describe the circumstances under which the defenses of intoxication, necessity, and duress would have the best chance of succeeding.

10. Describe the rules and issues surrounding self-defense and entrapment.

11. Discuss recent reforms of the criminal law.

KEY TERMS AND CONCEPTS

Mores
Folkways
Code of Hammurabi
Lex Talionis
Twelve Tables
Plebeians
Patricians
Wergild
Bot
Wer
Wite
Oath-Helpers
Shire
Hundreds
Tithings

Shire-gemot
Hali-gemot
Stare Decisis
Common Law
Inchoate crimes
Statutory crimes
Tort law
Felony
Misdemeanor
Mala in se
Mala prohibitum
Vagrancy
Actus reas
Mens rea
Transferred intent

Constructive intent
Strict liability
Ignorance or mistake
Insanity
M'Naghten rule
Irresistible impulse
Substantial capacity test
Intoxication
Duress
Necessity
Self-defense
Entrapment
Stalking
Community notification laws

NAMES TO KNOW

King Dungi
Hammurabi
William the Conqueror
Henry II
Edna Erez
Bankole Thompson
Jennifer Hoult
Oliver Wendell Holmes
William Chambliss
Jeffrey Adler
Daniel M'Naghten

Edward Drummond
Sir Robert Peel
Wayne LaFave
Austin Scott
John Hinckley
Ronald Reagan
Dudley and Stephens
Bernhard Goetz
Jacobsen
Jack Kevorkian
Megan Kanka

FILL-IN REVIEW

1. The _____ Code is not only the foundation of Judeo-Christian moral teachings, but it also is a basis for the U.S. legal system: prohibitions against murder, theft, perjury, and adultery precede by several thousand years the same laws found in the U.S. legal system.

2. The foundation of law in the United States is the English _____ law.

3. Before the Norman Conquest in 1066, the _____ were responsible for maintaining order among themselves and dealing with disturbances, fires, wild animals, etc.

4. If the act concerned in any way spiritual matters, it could be judged by clergymen and church officials in courts known as holy-motes or _____.

5. After the Norman Conquest in 1066, the church courts handled acts that might be considered sin, and the local hundred or manor courts (referred to as _____) dealt with most secular violations.

6. King Henry II used traveling judges, better known as _____ judges.

7. After <u>Rex v. Scofield</u>, attempt became a common-law crime, and today most U.S. jurisdictions have enacted some form of criminal attempt law (_____ crimes).

8. In a civil case, the defendant is required to pay damages if, by a _____ of the evidence, the trier of fact finds that the defendant committed the wrong.

9. A _____ is a civil action in which an individual asks to be compensated for personal harm.

10. A _____ is usually defined as a crime punishable by death or imprisonment for more than one year in a state prison, and a _____ as a crime punishable by less than a year in a local county jail or house of correction.

11. The _____ criminal law today is a written code defining crimes and their punishments.

12.   By delegating enforcement to others, the criminal law controls an individual's need to seek
       _____ or vengeance against those who violate his or her rights.

13.   <u>Mala in se</u> crimes such as murder and forcible rape are rooted in the core values inherent in
       Western civilization. Another type of crime, sometimes called statutory crime or _____
       _____ crimes, involves violations of laws that reflect current public opinion and social
       values such as drug use and possession of unlicensed guns.

14.   While violations of folkways and mores are controlled _____, breaches of the criminal
       law are left to the jurisdiction of political agencies.

15.   The power of the law to express norms and values can be viewed in the development of the crime of
       _____ (the "going about from place to place by a person without visible means of
       support, who is idle, and who, though able to work for his or her maintenance, refuses to do so, but
       lives without labor or on the charity of others").

16.   In most situations, for an act to constitute a crime, it must be performed with criminal intent---
       otherwise known as _____ _____. Intent in the legal sense can mean
       carrying out an act intentionally, knowingly, and willingly. However, the definition also
       encompasses situations in which recklessness or negligence establishes the required criminal intent.

17.   The _____ _____ Test allows the defense of insanity to be used for
       situations in which defendants were unable to control their behavior because of a mental disease.

18.   _____ is a defense to a crime when the defendant commits an illegal act because the
       defendant or a third person has been threatened by another with death or serious bodily harm if the
       act is not performed.

19.   As the famous English case <u>Regina v. Dudley and Stephens</u>, indicates _____ does not
       justify the intentional killing of another.

20.   The _____ defense is raised when the defendant maintains that law enforcement
       officers induced him or her to commit a crime.

21.   The state of Michigan is one of the few that allows prosecution under _____ .

22.   Dr. Kevorkian practices what he calls _____ .

TRUE/FALSE

1.   Crime and criminal behavior were recognized in many early societies.

2.   The criminal law is a static document which constantly resists with vigor any attempts to keep up
      with changing conditions and developments in society.

3.   As it is used today, the term common law refers to a law applicable to commoners in England.

4.   In a criminal action, the injured party must initiate proceedings by bringing charges and
      prosecuting the violator.

5.   Establishing guilt by a preponderance of the evidence is easier than establishing it beyond a reasonable doubt.

6.   A person can possibly be held both criminally and civilly liable for one action.

7.   In U.S. society, the state and federal governments have developed their own unique criminal codes.

8.   Every society maintains unwritten rules of conduct.

9.   Few legal systems are designed to support and maintain the boundaries of the socio-economic system they serve.

10. William Chambliss finds that early English vagrancy laws were less concerned with maintaining capitalism than with controlling children and relieving the overburdened public relief and juvenile systems.

11. To fulfill the legal definition of a crime, all elements of the crime must be proven.

12. Thoughts of committing an illegal act constitute a crime.

13. The central issue concerning voluntariness is whether the individual has control over his or her actions.

14. A private citizen who sees a person drowning is under a legal obligation to save that person.

15. The underlying purpose of strict-liability laws is to protect the public.

16. Self-defense is a type of excuse defense.

17. As a general rule, ignorance of the law is an excuse.

18. As used in U.S. courts, insanity does not necessarily mean that persons using the defense are mentally ill or unbalanced.

19. The Substantial Capacity Test is essentially a combination of the M'Naghten Rule and the Irresistible Impulse Test.

20. Most successful insanity verdicts result in the accused being discharged back into the community.

21. Evidence shows that most insanity defense pleas are successful.

22. Intoxication is generally not considered a defense.

23. Duress is a defense when defendants commit a serious crime such as murder to save themselves or others.

24. The use of deadly force is considered reasonable to protect private property.

14

MULTIPLE CHOICE

1. Which of the following is associated with the origin of the jury trial:
    a. in early medieval Europe and England, disputed criminal charges were often decided by the parties in an athletic contest which took place on a "level playing field"
    b. since the time of William the Conqueror, twelve knights in each district were called before an "inquest" of the king's justices to give local tax information
    c. except for crimes committed in shires, a group of freemen acted as witnesses who told the judges what they considered were public wrongs against the crown
    d. none of the above is associated with the origin of the jury trial ("a" thru "c")

2. Common law is:
    a. law created by legislatures
    b. law decided by juries
    c. law of the land in England
    d. law for common people

3. Which of the following is <u>true</u> about drug or drug laws:
    a. they were drafted by appellate court judges to reflect existing social and economic conditions in the nineteenth century
    b. the use of narcotics became habits of the middle class early in the nation's history,
    c. these statutes helped focus attention on inchoate narcotics acts to protect the poor from the demands of the industrial age
    d. public and governmental concern arose over the use of narcotics by northern Europeans who had come to the United States to build railroads and work in mines

4. The successful defense in the case of Jacobson versus U.S., used the defense of:
    a. necessity
    b. duress
    c. entrapment
    d. ignorance

5. Tort law refers to:
    a. the law of personal wrongs and damage
    b. the law governing transfer and ownership of property
    c. the law of personal agreements
    d. the law of harm to society

6. A <u>mala in se</u> offense:
    a. marijuana possession
    b. gambling
    c. forcible rape
    d. none of the above ("a" thru "c")

7. A case in which an English court ruled that a merchant who held and transported merchandise for another was guilty of theft if he kept the goods for his own purposes:
    a. <u>Penn's Case</u>
    b. <u>Henry's Case</u>
    c. <u>Carrier's Case</u>
    d. none of the above ("a" thru "c")

8.   Jeffery Adler argues that early English _____ laws were less concerned with maintaining capitalism than with controlling beggars and relieving the overburdened public relief and welfare system.
       a.   vagrancy
       b.   "blue"
       c.   "symbolic"
       d.   economic
       e.   none of the above ("a" thru "d")

9.   A legal duty to act is dependent on such common situations as:
       a.   the relationship of parties based on status
       b.   imposition by statute
       c.   contractual relationship
       d.   both "a" and "c" are true
       e.   all of the above ("a" thru "c") are true

10.   If Dan breaks into and enters Emily's house but has no intent to commit a crime once inside, he cannot be convicted of burglary because he lacked _____ intent.
       a.   exact
       b.   precise
       c.   definite
       d.   specific
       e.   distinctive

11.   The intent that underlies the finding of criminal liability for an unintentional act is known as _____ intent.
       a.   transferred
       b.   constructive
       c.   accidental
       d.   broad

12.   A strict-liability crime:
       a.   arson
       b.   larceny
       c.   health regulations
       d.   malentendu

13.   Which of the follow is a type of excuse defense:
       a.   insanity
       b.   self defense
       c.   castle doctrine
       d.   both "b" and "c" are types of excuse defenses
       e.   all of the above are types of excuse defenses ("a" thru "c")

14.   In 1843, the English court established the _____ Rule, also known as the right-wrong test.
       a.   Mind Disease
       b.   Elizabeth
       c.   Peel
       d.   M'Naghten
       e.   Durham

15. A plea in which defendants serve the first of their sentence in a hospital, and once "cured," serve the remaining portion in a prison:
    a. not guilty by reason of insanity
    b. not guilty in lieu of insanity
    c. guilty but insane
    d. guilty but mentally ill

16. It is estimated that the insanity plea is used in fewer than _____ percent of all cases.
    a. one
    b. five
    c. ten
    d. twenty-five

17. The defense of _____ is applied in situations in which a person must break the law in order to avoid a greater evil caused by natural physical forces.
    a. necessity
    b. duress
    c. coercion
    d. reasonableness

18. A defense used to protect one's person or one's property:
    a. necessity
    b. duress
    c. self-defense
    d. entrapment
    e. intoxication

19. The insanity plea was thrust into the spotlight when _____ _____ attempted to kill President Ronald Reagan.
    a. Moses Norman
    b. Edwin Sutherland
    c. Edward Drummond
    d. John Hinckley

20. Community notification laws emerged as a response to concerns about:
    a. burglars
    b. pornography
    c. gangs
    d. sexual predators

21. The self-defense concept received national publicity when, on December 22, 1984, _____ shot four would-be robbers on a subway in New York.
    a. Waltham Black
    b. Harrison Thompson
    c. Robert Peel
    d. Bernhard Goetz
    e. Scott LaFave

MATCHING

____	1.	Local nobleman	A.	To stand by decided cases
____	2.	Common law	B.	Traffic law
____	3.	Sierra Leone	C.	Roman law
____	4.	Civil law	D.	Compensation
____	5.	lex talionis	E.	Hali-gemot
____	6.	Stare decisis	F.	Lesser of two evils
____	7.	Mala prohibitum	G.	Private wrong
____	8.	Actus reus	H.	Judge-made law
____	9.	Twelve Tables	I.	An eye for an eye
____	10.	Insanity	J.	Irresistible Impulse
____	11.	Necessity	K.	Guilty act
____	12.	Wergild	L.	"Woman-damage"

ESSAY QUESTIONS

1. Describe the various components of the legal system in England prior to the Norman Conquest in 1066.

2. Trace the origins and early development of the common law.

3. Compare common law to statutory law.

4. Explain the differences and similarities between criminal and civil law.

5. Briefly discuss the differences between felonies and misdemeanors.

6. Identify and describe the functions of the criminal law.

7. Compare the views of Chambliss and Adler toward vagrancy laws.

8. Describe the two types of actus reus.

9. What is the difference between general intent and specific intent?

10. What do transferred intent and constructive intent mean?

11. Is ignorance of the law a legitimate excuse to criminal liability? Explain.

12. Compare the M'Naghten Rule to the Irresistible Impulse Test.

13. Why is there so much controversy over the insanity defense? How have some states responded to the controversy?

14. What are the differences between the defense of necessity and duress?

15. Identify and describe the kind of circumstances in which self-defense would be considered reasonable and necessary.

CHAPTER TWO ANSWER SECTION

FILL-IN REVIEW

1.	Mosaic		12.	retribution
2.	common		13.	mala prohibitum
3.	tithings		14.	informally
4.	ecclesiastics		15.	vagrancy
5.	court-leet		16.	mens rea
6.	circuit		17.	Irresistible Impulse
7.	inchoate		18.	duress
8.	preponderance		19.	necessity
9.	tort		20.	entrapment
10.	felony; misdemeanor		21.	common law
11.	substantive		22.	Obitiatry

TRUE/FALSE

1.	T	13.	T
2.	F	14.	F
3.	F	15.	T
4.	F	16.	F
5.	T	17.	F
6.	T	18.	T
7.	T	19.	T
8.	T	20.	F
9.	F	21.	F
10.	F	22.	T
11.	T	23.	F
12.	F	24.	F

MULTIPLE CHOICE

1.	b	12.	c
2.	c	13.	a
3.	b	14.	d
4.	c	15.	c
5.	a	16.	a
6.	c	17.	a
7.	c	18.	c
8.	a	19.	d
9.	e	20.	d
10.	d	21.	d
11.	b		

MATCHING

1.	E
2.	H
3.	L
4.	G
5.	I
6.	A
7.	B
8.	K
9.	C
10.	J
11.	F
12.	D

3 _The Nature and Extent of Crime_

LEARNING OBJECTIVES

1. Compare and contrast the nature, purposes, findings, and problems of the Uniform Crime report, self-report surveys, and victim surveys.

2. Describe recent crime trends in the United States.

3. Discuss the relationship between firearms and interpersonal violence.

4. Describe the controversies surrounding the relationship between crime and social class.

5. Describe the conflicting findings about the relationship between crime and age.

6. Compare early and late views of gender differences in the crime rate.

7. Explain the factors associated with violent crime among African Americans.

8. Describe the problem of the career criminal.

9. Describe the nature and importance of those cohort studies which focus on chronic offenders.

10. Identify the effect of the chronic offender on criminal justice system policy.

KEY TERMS AND CONCEPTS

Uniform crime Report
UCR.
Index crimes
Type I crimes
Type II crimes
Self-report survey
National crime victimization survey
NCVS
Crime patterns and trends
Monitoring the future
Yakuza
Bosozoku

Instrumental crime
Expressive crime
Aging out
Desistance phenomenon
Masculinity hypothesis
Chivalry hypothesis
Androgens
Liberal Feminist theory
Criminal careers
Chronic offender
Continuity of crime
Early onset criminality

NAMES TO KNOW

Patrick Jackson	John Hinckley	Richard Herrnstein
John Clark	David McDowall	Cesare Lombroso
Larry Tifft	Colin Loftin	Freda Adler
Michael Hindelang	Brian Wiersma	Rita James Simon
Travis Hirschi	Gary Kleck	Roy Austin
Joseph Weis	Chester Britt	Leroy Gould
Terence Thornberry	David Bordua	Harwin Voss
Thomas Gray	David Lester	Ronald Akers
Eric Wish	James Short	James P. Comer
Joseph Sheley	F. Ivan Nye	Charles Silberman
James Wright	Charles Tittle	Gary LaFree
Darrell Steffensmeier	Wayne Villemez	Marvin Wolfgang
Miles Harer	Douglas Smith	Robert Figlio
James A. Fox	Robert Meier	Thorsten Sellin
Rosemary Gartner	David Brownfield	Lyle Shannon
Robert Nash Parker	Sally Simpson	D. J. West
John Braithwaite	Lori Elis	D. P. Farrington
Ellen Cohn	Travis Hirschi	Paul Tracy
James Rotton	Michael Gottfredson	Kimberly Kempf-Leonard
James Brady	Gordon Trasler	David Farrington
Ronald Reagan	James Q. Wilson	J. David Hawkins

FILL-IN REVIEW

1. The accuracy of the UCR has been heavily criticized. The three greatest areas of concern are _____ practices, law enforcement practices, and methodological problems.

2. One alternative to official statistics and victim surveys is the _____ survey.

3. Used to test the validity of self-reports, _____ method compares incarcerated youths with "normal" groups to see whether the former report more delinquency.

4. The _____ _____ Survey is conducted today by the U.S. Bureau of the Census in cooperation with the Bureau of Justice Statistics of the U.S. Department of Justice.

5. The postwar _____ generation reached their teenage years in the 1960s, just as the violent crime rate began a sharp increase.

6. Those unable to obtain desired goods and services through conventional means may consequently resort to theft and other illegal activities to obtain them; these activities are referred to as _____ crime.

7. Travis Hirschi and Michael Gottfredson maintain that the relationship between age and crime is _____, and therefore, the age variable is actually irrelevant to the study of crime.

8. If the relationship between age and crime varies, it would be necessary to conduct _____ studies which follow criminals over their life cycle in order to fully understand how their age influences their offending patterns.

9. Why does the crime rate decline with age? One view is that there is a direct relationship between aging and _____. As they mature, troubled youths are able to develop a long-term life view and resist the need for immediate gratification.

10. Wilson and Herrnstein argue that the aging out process is a function of the _____ _____ of the human life cycle.

11. Lombroso's theory of female criminality is called the _____ _____.

12. Referred to as the _____ _____, this view holds that much of the criminality of women is masked because of the generally protective and benevolent attitudes towards women in our culture.

13. By mid-century it was common for criminologists to portray gender differences in the crime rate as a function of _____.

14. Adler and Simon's research is referred to today as _____ feminist theory, an approach which focused attention on the social and economic role of women in society.

15. Self-report studies suggest that the delinquent behavior rates of African American and White teenagers are generally similar, and that differences in _____ statistics may indicate a differential selection policy by police.

16. Comer's view fits well with the criminological concept that a subculture of _____ has developed in inner-city ghetto areas which condone the use of physical force as a solution for everyday encounters.

17. Moving to northern cities, African Americans suffered two burdens unknown to other migrants: their color and their heritage of _____.

18. Farrington finds that the most important childhood risk factors associated with chronic offending include a history of troublesomeness, a _____ which reveres daring behavior, a delinquent sibling and a convicted parent.

19. Some criminologists view African American crime as a function of _____ in a society where the African American family and culture was torn apart in such a way that recovery has proven impossible.

20. Wolfgang used official records to follow the criminal careers of a _____ of 9,945 boys born in Philadelphia.

TRUE/FALSE

1. The major unit of analysis in the Uniform Crime Report involves index crimes or Type I crimes.

2. The methods used to compile the UCR are quite simple.

3. Property crimes are more likely to be solved than violent crimes.

4. Police efficiency and professionalism may help increase crime rates.

5.   No federal crimes are reported in the Uniform Crime Report.

6.   It is quite apparent that the number of crimes reported to the FBI is considerably larger than the number of crimes accounted for by the NCVS.

7.   Large rural areas have the highest violence rates.

8.   Most guns used in crime are obtained illegally.

9.   Official statistics indicate that crime rates in inner-city, high-poverty areas are generally higher than those in suburban or wealthier areas.

10.   The weight of recent evidence seems to suggest that serious and/or official crime is no more prevalent among the lower classes.

11.   Age is inversely related to criminality.

12.   The three major forms of criminal statistics generally agree that male crime rates are considerably higher than those of females.

13.   Early criminological literature paid great attention to female criminals.

14.   African-Americans are arrested for a disproportionate amount of violent crime such as robbery and murder.

15.   Black violence rates are much lower in other nations, both those which are predominantly white, such as Canada, and those which are predominantly black, such as Nigeria.

16.   Wolfgang found that arrest and court experience did much to deter the chronic recidivist.

17.   Today, the chronic offender is a central focus of criminal justice system policy.

MULTIPLE CHOICE

1.   The best known and most widely cited source of aggregate criminal statistics:
      a.   National Crime Survey
      b.   Uniform Crime Report
      c.   Bureau of Justice Statistics
      d.   Index Crime Data

2.   Which of the following is a Type I crime:
      a.   embezzlement
      b.   kidnapping
      c.   auto theft
      d.   prostitution
      e.   white collar crime

3.	Traditionally, about _____ percent of all reported index crimes are cleared by arrest.
	a.	one
	b.	five
	c.	ten
	d.	twenty
	e.	forty

4.	When the UCR indicates that the murder rate was 8.2 in 1995, it means that about 8.2 people in every _____ experienced murder between January 1 and December 31 of 1995.
	a.	1,000
	b.	10,000
	c.	100,000
	d.	1,000,000

5.	The first national survey of 10,000 households was conducted in 1966 through the sponsorship of the _____ Commission.
	a.	President's
	b.	Knapp
	c.	Warren
	d.	Nixon

6.	It has been estimated that almost _____ percent of all youths commit delinquent and criminal acts.
	a.	10
	b.	20
	c.	30
	d.	60
	e.	90

7.	Most reported crimes occur during the months of _____.
	a.	January and February
	b.	March and April
	c.	May and June
	d.	July and August
	e.	September and October

8.	The _____ states now have the dubious distinction of having the highest crime and violence rate.
	a.	Northern
	b.	Western
	c.	Southern
	d.	Eastern

9.	Handguns are the cause of death for _____ of all police killed in the line of duty.
	a.	one quarter
	b.	one third
	c.	half
	d.	two thirds
	e.	three quarter

10. National surveys of adolescents, including one conducted in 1993 for the Harvard School of Public Health, have found that up to _____ percent of all students report carrying a gun to school and 13 percent had been threatened with gun violence.
    a. 5
    b. 15
    c. 25
    d. 35

11. The _____ Gun Control Act of 1968 prohibits dealers from selling guns to minors, ex-felons, and drug users.
    a. Federal
    b. State
    c. Brady
    d. none of the above ("a" thru "c").

12. The most famous attempt to regulate handguns is the Massachusetts Bartley-Fox Law, which provides a mandatory _____ prison term for possession of a handgun (outside the home).
    a. six month
    b. one-year
    c. five-year
    d. ten-year

13. Which of the following is true about the re-assessment of the concept of the "new female criminal":
    a. the emancipation of women has had an important influence on female crime rates
    b. many female criminals come from the socioeconomic class least effected by the women's movement
    c. the offense patterns of women are quite similar to those of men
    d. the gender-crime association was affected by cultural changes during the last fifty years

14. The Uniform Crime Report (UCR) arrest statistics indicate that the overall male-female arrest ratio is usually about _____ male offenders to one female offender.
    a. two
    b. four
    c. eight
    d. ten
    e. twelve

15. _____ argued that whereas women generally were more passive and less criminal than men, there was a small group of female criminals who lacked "typical" female traits of "piety, maternity, underdeveloped intelligence, and weakness."
    a. Delbert Elliott
    b. John Laub
    c. Martin Gold
    d. Cesare Lombroso

16.   The work of Charles Silberman suggests that African American violence is a result of
        _____.
        a.   demographic factors
        b.   early school problems
        c.   anthropological encounters with police culture
        d.   the African American experience in this country

17.   The most well-known discovery of Wolfgang and his associates was that of the so-called
        _____ offender.
        a.   persistent
        b.   reluctant
        c.   aggressive
        d.   assertive
        e.   chronic

MATCHING

____ 1.   Index crime   A.   Desistance phenomenon
____ 2.   Victim surveys   B.   Fear of punishment
____ 3.   Brady Bill   C.   African American experience
____ 4.   Rape   D.   Expressive crime
____ 5.   "Aging out"   E.   The Female Offender
____ 6.   Glassner & associates   F.   Larceny
____ 7.   Cesare Lombroso   G.   Gun control
____ 8.   Rita J. Simon   H.   Liberal feminist theory
____ 9.   Charles Silberman   I.   "Dark figure of crime"
____ 10. Marvin Wolfgang   J.   Philadelphia cohort study

ESSAY QUESTIONS

1.   Identify and discuss the two ways crimes are cleared.

2.   Describe the three ways used to express crime data in the Uniform Crime Report.

3.   Describe how law enforcement practices and methodological problems adversely affect the accuracy of the UCR.

4.   How would police interpretation of the definitions of index crimes affect reporting practices?

5.   Describe the three changes that were initiated recently in the Uniform Crime Reports.

6.   Why have most self-report studies focused on juvenile delinquency and youth crime?

7.   What are the advantages of using self-report studies? What are the problems with this approach?

8.   How is the National Crime Survey administered?

9.   Describe the methodological problems with the National Crime Survey.

10. Describe the similarities and differences in findings among the three methods of collecting criminal statistics.

11. Is the crime rate going up in the U.S.? Explain.

12. What are some possible reasons for the much lower crime rate in Japan?

13. What are the reasons most often given by victims for not reporting crime?

14. What are some possible reasons for the most recent increases in reported violent crime?

15. What have been the results of laws that punish the use of handguns in crime?

16. Describe the conflicting research findings on the relationship between crime and both social class and age.

17. Describe the Hirschi/Gottfredson view toward the relationship between crime and age.

18. What is the relationship, if any, between the women's movement and female criminality?

19. Describe James P. Comer's views of the factors underlying African American violence.

20. Describe Silberman's perspective on how the African American experience has resulted in black violence.

21. Describe the meaning and importance of Marvin Wolfgang's chronic recidivist studies.

CHAPTER THREE ANSWER SECTION

FILL-IN REVIEW

1.	reporting	11.	masculinity hypothesis
2.	self-report	12.	chivalry hypothesis
3.	known group	13.	socialization
4.	National Crime	14.	liberal
5.	"baby boom"	15.	arrest
6.	instrumental	16.	violence
7.	constant	17.	slavery
8.	longitudinal	18.	personality
9.	desistance	19.	socialization
10.	natural history	20.	cohort

TRUE/FALSE

1.	T	10.	F
2.	F	11.	T
3.	F	12.	T
4.	T	13.	F
5.	T	14.	T
6.	F	15.	T
7.	F	16.	F
8.	T	17.	T
9.	T		

MULTIPLE CHOICE

1.	b	10.	b
2.	c	11.	a
3.	d	12.	b
4.	c	13.	b
5.	a	14.	b
6.	e	15.	d
7.	d	16.	d
8.	b	17.	e
9.	d		

MATCHING

1.	F
2.	I
3.	G
4.	D
5.	A
6.	B
7.	E
8.	H
9.	C
10.	J

4   *Victims and Victimization*

LEARNING OBJECTIVES

1.   Describe the various costs of becoming a crime victim.

2.   Explain the patterns and social ecology of victimization.

3.   Describe the factors associated with households that contain crime victims.

4.   Compare social and demographic features which differentiate victims from non-victims.

5.   Identify the characteristics of offenders who come into contact with victims through such crimes as rape, assault and robbery.

6.   Explain the type of offenders who commit parricide.

7.   Describe the meaning and importance of victim precipitation in explaining violent criminal acts.

8.   Explain how one's lifestyle influences the probability of becoming a victim.

9.   Explain how the routine activities approach is helpful in understanding variations in the crime rate.

10.   Compare the equivalent group hypothesis to the proximity hypothesis.

11.   Identify and describe the most important and common victim assistance programs.

12.   Describe some suggested changes that might foster a better relationship between the victim and the criminal justice system.

13.   Describe the value and impact of target hardening and victim resistance measures.

KEY TERMS AND CONCEPTS

Victimology
Anti-social behavior
Cycle of violence
Social ecology of victimization
Parricide
Victim precipitation
Active precipitation

Passive precipitation
Life-style theory
Equivalent group hypothesis
Proximity hypothesis
Deviant place hypothesis
Routine activities theory
Suitable targets
Capable guardians

Motivated offenders
Victim compensation
Victim-offender reconciliation
Victim's rights
Victim advocacy
Crisis intervention
Target hardening

NAMES TO KNOW

Tim Ireland
Cathy Spatz Widom
Richard Gelles
Murray Straus
Eric and Lyle Menendez
Kathleen Heide
Richard Jahnke
Deborah Jahnke
Jonathan Cantero
Michelle White
John White Jr.
Stephen Schafer
Hans Von Hentig
Marvin Wolfgang
Menachim Amir
Susan Estrich

Steven Lord
Rosemary Gartner
Bill McCarthy
Gary Jensen
David Brownfield
Kevin Fitzpatrick
Mark La Gory
Ferris Ritchey
Joan McDermott
Simon Singer
Elise Lake
Pamela Wilcox Rountree
Kenneth Land
Terence Miethe
Lawrence Cohen
Marcus Felson

Robert Meier
Steven Messner
Kenneth Tardiff
James Lasley
Christopher Birkbeck
Gary Lafree
James Massey
Leslie Kennedy
Stephen Baron
Dean Kilpatrick
Ronald Reagan
Andrew Karmen
Frank Carrington
Polly Marchbanks
Gary Kleck
Gary Green

FILL-IN REVIEW

1. Those criminologists who focus their attention on the crime victim refer to themselves as _____.

2. The _____ _____ Crime Survey is the leading source of information today about the nature and extent of victimization.

3. Teens spend a great deal of time in one of the most dangerous places in the community: _____ _____ _____.

4. Young African-American males face a _____ risk five to eight times higher than that of young white males and 16 to 22 times higher than that of young white females.

5. _____ is the killing of a close relative.

6. _____ is the killing of a father.

7. _____ is the killing of a mother.

8. In the theory of _____ _____, victims actually initiated the confrontation which eventually led to their injury or death.

9. _____ rapes which may at first start out as a romantic though non-intimate relationship and then deteriorate into rape are rarely treated with the same degree of punitiveness as stranger rapes.

10. Some criminologists believe that people may become crime victims because they have a _____ which increases their exposure to criminal offenders.

11. Victimization _____ is increased by such behaviors as staying single, associating with young men, going out in public places late at night, and by living in an urban area.

12. _____ crimes are violent crimes against the person and crimes in which an offender attempts to steal an object directly.

13. Cohen and Felson argue that the number of adult caretakers at home during the day (called _____) decreased because of increased female participation in the work force.

14. The _____ hypothesis is based on the logical assumption that people who reside in so-called "high crime areas" have the greatest risk of coming into contact with criminal offenders irrespective of their own behavior or lifestyle.

15. The proximity hypothesis suggests that there may be _____ places in which crime flourishes.

16. More than half of victim programs provide _____ _____ to victims, many of whom are feeling isolated, vulnerable and in need of immediate services.

17. One way the self-protection trend has been manifested is in the concept of _____ _____ or making one's home and business crime proof through locks, bars, alarms, and other devices.

TRUE/FALSE

1. Victimization is random.

2. Higher income black households in Western urban areas are the most vulnerable to crime.

3. During their lifetime, 99 percent of the U.S. population will experience personal theft and 87 percent will become a theft victim three or more times.

4. Gender is related to one's chances of being a victim of crime.

5. Older people face a much greater victimization risk than do younger persons.

6. Survey research showed that children suffer physical abuse from parents at a relatively low rate: the average number of assaults a child experienced per year was 2.5.

7. Passive precipitation occurs when the victim unknowingly threatens the attacker.

8. Whites were more than five times as likely to become robbery victims as African-Americans.

9. Crime tends to be interracial: blacks victimize whites, and whites victimize blacks.

10. There is a gender gap in intimate violence.

11. Killing of a parent is almost a daily event in the U.S.

12. Heide finds that public attitudes towards parricidal youth are changing from sympathy to horror.

13.	Both NCS data and UCR information can be interpreted as suggesting that the risk of being a crime victim is a function of personal characteristics and lifestyle.

14.	Research shows that teens may have the greatest risk of victimization.

15.	A variation of the lifestyle hypothesis is that victims and criminals do not share similar characteristics because they are in reality separate groups.

16.	Today victim compensation programs exist in only 20 states and the Federal government.

17.	Rape crisis centers typically feature twenty-four-hour-a-day emergency phone lines and information on police, medical, and court procedures.

18.	A recent Federal study of robbery victims found that victims who fought back were less likely to experience completed crimes than passive victims, but they were also more likely to be injured during the robbery.

19.	Neighborhood patrol and block watch programs have had a great effect on the crime rate.

MULTIPLE CHOICE

1.	The National Crime Survey indicates that the annual number of victimizations in America approaches _____ million incidents.
	a.	1
	b.	5
	c.	15
	d.	40

2.	In the aftermath of violence:
	a.	male victims tend to internalize and place the blame for their victimization on themselves
	b.	victims expressed feelings of being "weak" and "helpless" when viewing themselves from a "male frame" of reference
	c.	a crime such as rape costs its victims an average of $551,058.
	d.	female victims externalize blame, expressing anger toward their attackers

3.	Crimes of violence occurred most often:
	a.	in the late morning
	b.	in the late morning and early afternoon
	c.	in the late afternoon and early evening
	d.	in the evening
	e.	in the evening and early morning

4.	Those living in the _____ had significantly higher rates of theft and violence than those living in other places.
	a.	central city
	b.	suburbs
	c.	rural areas
	d.	none of the above

5.   The group least likely to become targets of theft offenses:
      a.   poor
      b.   rural
      c.   whites
      d.   from the northeast
      e.   all of the above ("a" thru "c")

6.   The probability of the average 12 year old being the victim of violent crime sometime is his or her
      life is about _____ percent.
      a.   26
      b.   55
      c.   83
      d.   92
      e.   99

7.   When men are the victim of violent crime the perpetrator is described as a(an)
      _____.
      a.   stranger
      b.   distant relative
      c.   acquaintance
      d.   close relative

8.   Victim risk diminishes rapidly after age _____.
      a.   15
      b.   25
      c.   35
      d.   45
      e.   55

9.   Which marital status group has the highest victimization risk:
      a.   unmarried
      b.   married
      c.   widows
      d.   widowers
      e.   none of the above ("a" thru "c")

10.   Which of the following is true about the victim and their criminal:
      a.   victims reported that a majority of crimes were committed by multiple offenders under the
            age of 20
      b.   about 25 percent of all violent crimes are committed by strangers
      c.   whites were the offenders in a majority of single-offender rapes and assault, but a majority
            of multiple-offender crimes involved black criminals
      d.   all of the above are true ("a" thru "c")

11.   While the focus of family violence usually falls on parents who injure children, it can also involve
      children who injure or kill parents;   about _____ people are killed by their children
      each year.
      a.   30
      b.   300
      c.   3,000
      d.   13,000

12. Nowhere is the concept of victim precipitation more controversial than in the crime of
_____.
   a. murder
   b. robbery
   c. prostitution
   d. rape
   e. assault

13. Cohen and Felson believe that predatory crime is closely related to:
   a. suitable targets
   b. capable guardians
   c. motivated offenders
   d. all of the above
   e. none of the above

14. National victim surveys indicate that almost every American age 12 and over will one day become the victim of common law crimes such as:
   a. larceny
   b. embezzlement
   c. extortion
   d. traffic violations

15. The Omnibus Victim and Witness Protection Act required:
   a. that in every criminal prosecution, the victim shall have the right to be present and to be heard at all critical stages of the judicial proceedings
   b. the use of victim impact statements at sentencing in Federal criminal cases
   c. protection of witnesses and victims from intimidation by prosecutors
   d. none of the above ("a" thru "c").

16. The number of victim-witness assistance programs that have developed in the United States is approximately:
   a. 20
   b. 200
   c. 2,000
   d. 20,000
   e. 200,000

17. No crime requires more crisis intervention efforts than _____.
   a. aggravated assault
   b. robbery
   c. extortion
   d. rape
   e. kidnapping

18. A finding of Gary Kleck's study of the effect of handgun ownership on victims:
   a. victims are rarely willing to use their guns against offenders
   b. victims injure family members more than offenders
   c. victims kill far more criminals than the police
   d. victim dissatisfaction with handguns result in their purchasing automatic assault rifles

34

19.   Polly Marchbanks and her associates found that fighting back:
   a.   helped community crime prevention programs
   b.   created fear of organized crime
   c.   both decreased the odds of a rape being completed and the victim's chances of injury
   d.   decreased the odds of a rape being completed but increased the victim's chances of injury
   e.   both increased the odds of a rape being completed and the victim's chances of injury

---

MATCHING

___	1.	Dangerous place	A.	Staying home at night
___	2.	Parricide	B.	Killing of a father
___	3.	Patricide	C.	Routine Activity Theory
___	4.	Life-style Theory	D.	Court services
___	5.	Marvin Wolfgang	E.	Public School
___	6.	Cohen & Felson	F.	Severely abused child
___	7.	Predatory crime	G.	Victim precipitation
___	8.	Victim assistance	H.	Violent crimes
		program		

ESSAY QUESTIONS

1.   Describe the suffering endured by crime victims after their attacker leaves the scene of the crime.

2.   Where, when, and how do most offenses occur according to NCS data?

3.   What factors are associated with households that contain crime victims?

4.   Based on NCS data, describe victims according to gender, age, race, social status, and marital status.

5.   What are some possible reasons for the high murder victimization rate of young black males?

6.   In Kathleen Heide's research on the nature of family homicides, she found that parricide is typically committed by one of three types of offenders. Identify and describe these three offender types.

7.   What is the importance of the work of Hans Von Hentig and Stephen Schafer?

8.   Describe victim-precipitated criminal homicide.

9.   What is the relationship between victim precipitation and rape?

10.   How does lifestyle influence victimization risk?

11.   How does the concept of "routine activities" help explain the rise in the crime rate since 1960?

12.   What is the relationship between the lifestyle view and the equivalent group hypothesis?

13.   Describe the recommendations of President Reagan's Task Force on Victims of Crime in 1982.

14. What did the Omnibus Victim and Witness Protection Act mandate?

15. What are victim compensation programs?

16. What court services are provided to victims?

17. What is the importance of the public education approach in victim programs?

18. Describe the services provided by rape crisis intervention programs.

19. What are some suggested changes that might enhance the relationship between the victim and the criminal justice system?

20. What self-protection methods have been employed?

21. How successful are victims when they fight back?

22. Does gun ownership for self-protection lower the crime rate? Explain.

CHAPTER FOUR ANSWER SECTION

FILL-IN REVIEW

1.	victimologists	10.	lifestyle
2.	National Victimization	11.	risk
3.	the public school	12.	Predatory
4.	murder	13.	guardians
5.	Parricide	14.	proximity
6.	Patricide	15.	deviant
7.	Matricide	16.	crisis intervention
8.	victim precipitation	17.	target hardening
9.	Date		

TRUE/FALSE

1.	F	11.	T
2.	T	12.	F
3.	T	13.	T
4.	T	14.	T
5.	F	15.	F
6.	F	16.	F
7.	T	17.	T
8.	F	18.	T
9.	F	19.	F
10.	T		

MULTIPLE CHOICE

1.	d	11.	b
2.	b	12.	d
3.	e	13.	d
4.	a	14.	a
5.	e	15.	b
6.	c	16.	c
7.	a	17.	d
8.	b	18.	c
9.	a	19.	d
10.	c		

MATCHING

1.	E
2.	F
3.	B
4.	A
5.	G
6.	C
7.	H
8.	D

5   Choice Theories

LEARNING OBJECTIVES

1.   Describe the development of and factors associated with choice theory.

2.   Define the concept of rational choice.

3.   Explain Ernest Van Den Haag's views toward the value of rehabilitation.

4.   Describe crime as both offense and offender specific.

5.   Describe potential crime reducing techniques.

6.   Define and describe the different types of deterrence.

7.   Identify and describe the contradictory findings of the three types of research on capital punishment: immediate impact studies, comparative research, and time series analysis.

8.   Explain the results of research measuring deterrent effects.

9.   Discuss the role of informal sanctions on reducing crime.

10.   Review the studies that support the idea that specific deterrence strategies can lessen crimes.

11.   Define the concept of selective incapacitation. Identify the problems with its use.

12.   Describe the weaknesses of an incapacitation approach to crime control.

13.   Highlight the theory of retribution and its modern version, just dessert.

KEY TERMS AND CONCEPTS

Rational choice
Classical criminology
Utilitarianism
Crime displacement
offender-specific crime
Routine activities
macro-view
micro-view
Suitable targets
Permeable neighborhoods
Capable guardians
Motivated criminals
Interactive effects

Peep game
Seductions of crime
Situational crime
prevention
General deterrence
Specific deterrence
Incapacitation strategies
Defensible space
Crime discouragers
Crime displacement
Extinction
Discouragement

Diffusion
Crackdowns
Time series analysis
Ultimate deterrent
Informal sanctions
Humiliation
Threat system
Pain versus Shame
Reintegrative shaming
Selective incapacitation
"Three strikes and you're out"
Just dessert

38

NAMES TO KNOW

Cesare Beccaria
Jeremy Bentham
Robert Martinson
Charles Murray
Louis Cox
James Q. Wilson
Allan Abrahamse
Robert Agnew
Neal Shover
Bruce Jacobs
Paul Cromwell
Garland White
Ronald Clarke
D. Wayne Osgood
Patricia Harris
Lisa Maher
Patricia Morgan
Karen Ann Joe
James Wright
Peter Rossi
Richard Felson
Steven Messner
Jack Katz
Oscar Newman
C. Ray Jeffrey
Ross Homel
Barbara Morse
Delbert Elliott
Nancy Levigne
Lorraine Green

Charles Tittle
Alan Rowe
Jiang Wu
Allen Liska
Edwin Zedlewski
David Bayley
Thomas Marvell
Carlisle Moody
Lawrence Sherman
Gary Green
H. Laurence Ross
Richard McCleary
Gary LaFree
Robert Dann
John Cochran
Mitchell Chamlin
Mark Seth
David Phillips
Steven Stack
Karl Schuessler
Thorsten Sellin
Walter Reckless
Derral Cheatwood
Dane Archer
Rosemary Gartner
Marc Beittel
Isaac Ehrlich
Steven Klepper
Daniel Nagin

Scott Decker
Eleni Apospori
Geoffrey Alpert
Raymond Paternoster
Harold Grasmick
Robert Bursik
Kirk Williams
Richard Hawkins
Ernest Van Den Haag
James Williams
Daniel Rodeheaver
David Weisburd
Elin Waring
Ellen Chayet
Richard Berk
Graeme Newman
John Braithwaite
Stephen Mugford
Mark Stafford
Mark Warr
David Greenberg
Shlomo Shinnar
Reuel Shinnar
Stephan Van Dine
Simon Dinitz
John Conrad
Peter Greenwood
Marc Mauer
Andrew Von Hirsch

FILL-IN REVIEW

1. Some argue that the decision to commit crime is a matter of personal and _____ _____, made after weighing the potential benefits and consequences of crime.

2. The view that crime, in all its different forms, is a matter of reasoned _____ originated in _____ Theory.

3. In Britain, philosopher Jeremy Bentham (1748-1833) helped popularize Becarria's views in his writings on _____. According to this view, actions are evaluated by their tendency to produce pleasure, and happiness and avoid pain.

4. That crime is _____ _____ refers to the fact that offenders will react selectively to the characteristics of particular offenses.

5. That crime is _____ _____ refers to the fact that criminals are not simply driven people who for one reason or another engage in random acts of anti-social behavior.

6. Garland White found that _____ neighborhoods, those with a greater than usual number of access streets from traffic arteries into the neighborhood, are the ones most likely to have high crime rates.

7. In 1973 Oscar Newman coined the term _____ space to signify that crime could be prevented or displaced through the use of architectural design.

8. Sociologist Jack Katz argues that there are in fact immediate benefits and rewards to criminality which he labels the "_____ of crime."

9. Beefed up police patrols in one area may shift crimes to a more vulnerable neighborhood. While crime _____ cannot be a solution to the general problem of crime, there is some evidence that deflection efforts can reduce crime or produce less serious offense patterns.

10. The theory of _____ _____ holds that crimes rates will be influenced and controlled by the threat of criminal punishment.

11. Some police attempts to deter crime have taken the form of _____, sudden changes in police activity designed to increase the communicated threat or actual certainty of punishment.

12. Since the _____ _____ is the ultimate legal deterrent, its failure to deter violent crime jeopardizes the validity of the entire deterrence theory concept.

13. Advanced econometric statistical analysis has been used to conduct _____ _____ analysis, a complex statistical technique which tells researchers how the murder rate changes when death penalty statutes are created or eliminated.

14. Dann's early research showed that executions may actually increase the likelihood of murder. William Bowers and Glenn Pierce labeled this the _____ effect which occurs when potential criminals model their behavior after state authorities: If the government can kill its enemies, so can they.

15. _____ sanctions occur when significant others such as parents, peers, neighbors, and teachers direct their disapproval, stigma, anger, and indignation toward an offender.

16. Greenwood found in his study of over 2,000 inmates that _____ incapacitation of chronic offenders could reduce the rate of robbery offenses 15 percent while actually lowering the number of offenders incarcerated for that crime by 5 percent.

17. The effects of _____ deterrence seem to be the greatest on people who believe they are certain to be arrested for a crime and certain to be punished if arrested.

18. Braithwaite argues that crime control can be better achieved through a policy of reintegrative _____. Here disapproval is extended to the offender's evil deed, while at the same time they are cast as a respected person who can be reaccepted by society.

19. Von Hirsch would suggest that the offender should not be treated as more (or less) _____ than is warranted by the character of his or her offense.

40

20. A strict _____ policy may result in people being kept in prison beyond the time they are a threat to society while a new cohort of high risk adolescents is on the street.

21. It is the ideas and writings of _____ which inspire criminologists who believe that criminals choose to commit crime and that crime can be controlled by the judicious application of criminal punishments.

TRUE/FALSE

1. By the end of the nineteenth century, the popularity of the classical approach began to increase, and by the mid-twentieth century, the perspective was embraced by mainstream criminologists.

2. James Q. Wilson argues that while incapacitating criminals should not be the sole goal of the justice system, such a policy does have the advantage of restraining offenders and preventing their future criminality without having to figure out how to change or alter their attitude or nature, a goal which has proven difficult to accomplish.

3. Criminals tend to realistically estimate the money they earn from crime.

4. Rational choice theory dovetails with routine activities theory.

5. Studies of residential burglary indicate that criminals will forego activity if they believe a neighborhood is well patrolled by police.

6. Nail Shover found that older criminals may turn from a life of crime when they develop a belief that the risk of crime is greater than its potential profit.

7. Victimization data obtained by the NC indicates that low income households ($10,000 or less) are the most likely target of property crimes.

8. The focus of rational choice theory is on the criminal and not the opportunity to commit crime.

9. Corner homes, usually near traffic lights or stop signs, are the ones most likely to be burglarized.

10. Green showed that a deterrent strategy may work to respond to those using an illegal unauthorized descrambler to obtain pay cable programs.

11. The Kansas City study revealed that variations in patrol techniques had a great effect on the crime patterns.

12. Katz finds that situational inducements created from emotional upheaval can structure the decision to commit crime.

13. Two pioneering studies by Thorsten Sellin and Walter Reckless showed that there was little difference in the murder rates of adjacent states, regardless of their use of the death penalty..

14. An evaluation of executions in the United States by Steven Stack concluded that capital punishment does have immediate negative impact and that 16 well-publicized executions may have caused 480 additional murders.

15.	Research measuring the association between perceptions of punishment and behavior indicate that the severity and not the certainty of punishment may have a deterrent effect on behavior.

16.	Those people who believe apprehension will almost always result in harsh punishments will be the most likely to avoid the risk of criminal behavior.

17.	Empirical evidence indicates that the placement of steering locks has not helped reduce car theft in the United States.

18.	There is evidence from Britain that efforts to control drunk driving failed to produce a moral climate to diminish the incidence of drunk driving.

19.	Barbara Morse and Delbert Elliott found that installing a locking device on cars which prevents inebriated drivers from starting the vehicle significantly reduced drunk driving rates.

20.	Research on the benefits of incapacitation has shown that increasing the number of people behind bars can effectively reduce crime.

21.	Dessert theory is concerned with the rights of the accused.

22.	Research in 14 nations around the world found little evidence that countries with a death penalty have lower violence rates than those without; homicide rates actually decline after capital punishment is abolished.

23.	Researchers have found that people who have been caught and sanctioned subsequently lower their estimates of the risk involved in law violations.

MULTIPLE CHOICE

1.	Beginning in the mid-_____, the classical approach began to enjoy a resurgence of popularity. The rehabilitation of known criminals came under attack, while solutions to the crime problem which held that potential and actual criminals would "go straight" if they would learn to fear punishment became favored.
	a.	1890s
	b.	1940s
	c.	1970s
	d.	1980s

2.	Ernest Van Den Haag believes that the purpose of the law and justice system is to create a

	_____.
	a.	"threat system"
	b.	"defense system"
	c.	"treatment system"
	d.	none of the above ("a" thru "c")

3.   In 1973 Oscar Newman coined the term defensible space to signify that crime could be prevented or displaced through the use of:
     a.   psychological strategies
     b.   geographical patterns
     c.   regional barriers
     d.   architectural design

4.   "Street crimes" may be the product of careful analysis of _____ _____ including environmental, social, and structural factors.
     a.   risk assessment
     b.   strategic balance
     c.   rational overview
     d.   none of the above ("a" thru "c")

5.   Ronald Clarke and Patricia Harris find that auto thieves are very selective in their choice of targets. If they want to "strip" cars for their parts they are most likely to "choose"
     _____ .
     a.   Toyota Camry
     b.   Volkswagens
     c.   Buick Rivera
     d.   Camaro

6.   Charles Tittle and Alan Rowe found that if police are able to make an arrest in at least _____ of all reported crimes, the crime rate would significantly decline.
     a.   10 percent
     b.   30 percent
     c.   60 percent
     d.   90 percent

7.   One approach to testing deterrence theory is to set up actual _____ to see if subjects respond to the threat of legal sanctions.
     a.   measurements
     b.   investigations
     c.   pilots
     d.   experiments

8.   Perhaps the most famous experiment to evaluate the general effect of the threat of legal sanctions was conducted by the:
     a.   New York City Bureau of Trial Courts
     b.   Boston Transit Authority
     c.   Los Angeles Sheriff Department
     d.   Kansas City, Missouri Police Department
     e.   Chicago Housing Authority

9.   Isaac Ehrlich's 1975 research on capital punishment found that:
     a.   an average of 4.4 more homicides occurred during the sixty days following an execution than during those preceding it
     b.   16 well-publicized executions may have saved 480 lives
     c.   homicide rates declined in more than half the countries studied after abolition
     d.   each additional execution per year would save seven or eight people from being victims of murder

10. James Wright and Peter Rossi found that about _____ of all violent felons they surveyed were more afraid of armed victims than police; about 40 percent had avoided a victim because they believed they were armed, and almost one-third reported that they had been scared off, wounded or captured by armed victims.
    a. 60 percent
    b. 30 percent
    c. 10 percent
    d. 90 percent

11. Surveys show that approximately _____ percent of all offenders are substance abusers.
    a. 14
    b. 30
    c. 70
    d. 89
    e. 99

12. In Robert Dann's 1935 study in Philadelphia, he found that an average of _____ homicides occurred during the 60 days following an execution than during those preceding it.
    a. 12.6 more
    b. 4.4 more
    c. 12.6 fewer
    d. 4.4 fewer
    e. none of the above ("a" thru "c")

13. David Phillips studied the immediate effect of executions in Britain from 1858 to 1914 and found a _____ deterrent effect based on the publicity following the execution.
    a. regression
    b. retrospective
    c. temporary
    d. suppression

14. Sherman and Berk examined the effect of police action on domestic dispute cases and found that _____ percent of the arrested group repeated their violent behavior, while _____ percent of the advised group and _____ percent of the sent away group repeated their offenses.
    a. 45; 35; 10
    b. 34; 30; 49
    c. 40; 60; 20
    d. 10; 19; 24

15. In a famous statement _____ _____ conceded that "wicked people exist" and they must be separated from the law abiding.
    a. Peter Greenwood
    b. James Q. Wilson
    c. Graeme Newman
    d. Samuel Walker
    e. Douglas Smith

44

16. David Greenberg found that if the prison population were cut in half, the crime rate would most likely go up _____ percent; if prisons were entirely eliminated, crime might increase _____ percent.
    a. 4; 8
    b. 24; 28
    c. 44; 48
    d. 64; 68
    e. 84; 88

17. The just desert model suggests that:
    a. punishment based on deterrence is appropriate
    b. punishment should be the same for all people who commit the same crime
    c. criminal sentences based on individual needs or characteristics are fair
    d. none of the above ("a" thru "c")

MATCHING

____ 1. Mid-eighteenth century
____ 2. Mid-twentieth century
____ 3. Crime
____ 4. Defensible space
____ 5. Capable guardians
____ 6. Celerity
____ 7. Aggregate data source
____ 8. Suitable targets
____ 9. Diffusion effect
____ 10. James Q. Wilson
____ 11. Graeme Newman
____ 12. Andrew Von Hirsch

A. Architectural design
B. Speed
C. An event
D. Classical theory
E. Empty carport
F. "Nosy neighbors"
G. Positivism
H. Punishment works
I. Discouragement
J. Just desert
K. Uniform Crime Report
L. Acute corporal punishment

ESSAY QUESTIONS

1. What are the historical roots of choice theory?

2. What factors encouraged the emergence of choice theory?

3. Describe the concept of rational choice.

4. What are Ernest Van Den Haag's views of rehabilitation?

5. How can crime be both offense- and offender-specific?

6. How do offenders choose their targets?

7. Describe the evidence that shows that crimes are products of a rational decision process.

8. How do the factors of severity, certainty, and celerity relate to each other and to general deterrence?

9.   Describe the methodology and results of the Kansas City police study.

10.   Describe the findings of studies which examined the immediate impact of an execution on the murder rate.

11.   What were the findings of Issac Ehrlich's work on capital punishment?

12.   Describe the results of comparative research to time series studies of the death penalty.

13.   Under what kind of conditions will perceptual deterrence seem to have the greatest effect?

14.   What are the problems with panel studies?

15.   Explain the importance of informal sanctions.

16.   What are the problems with general deterrence theory?

17.   Describe Graeme Newman's provocative proposals for punishing offenders.

18.   What are the advantages and disadvantages of the concept of selective incapacitation?

19.   Identify the findings of David Greenberg's research on incapacitation. What policy implications flow from his research?

20.   What are the problems with the incapacitation strategy?

21.   What are Andrew Von Hirsch's views toward the concept of desert? How does desert theory deal with the rights of the accused?

46

CHAPTER FIVE ANSWER SECTION

FILL-IN REVIEW

1.	rational choice	12.	death penalty
2.	choice; classical	13.	time series
3.	utilitarianism	14.	brutalization
4.	"offense specific"	15.	Informal
5.	"offender specific"	16.	selective
6.	permeable	17.	perceptual
7.	defensible	18.	shaming
8.	seductions	19.	blameworthy
9.	displacement	20.	incarceration
10.	general deterrence	21.	Beccaria
11.	crackdowns		

TRUE/FALSE

1.	F	13.	T
2.	T	14.	F
3.	F	15.	F
4.	T	16.	T
5.	T	17.	F
6.	T	18.	F
7.	F	19.	T
8.	F	20.	F
9.	T	21.	T
10.	T	22.	T
11.	F	23.	T
12.	T		

MULTIPLE CHOICE

1.	c	10.	a
2.	a	11.	c
3.	d	12.	b
4.	a	13.	c
5.	b	14.	d
6.	b	15.	b
7.	d	16.	a
8.	d	17.	b
9.	d		

MATCHING

1.	D
2.	G
3.	C
4.	A
5.	F
6.	B
7.	K
8.	E
9.	I
10.	H
11.	L
12.	J

6   Trait Theories

LEARNING OBJECTIVES

1. Compare sociobiology to early theories of behavior.

2. Describe the general assumptions and approaches of biosocial theory.

3. Discuss the relationships between various biochemical factors and violent behavior.

4. Define the meaning and importance of electroencephalographs.

5. Outline the relationships between neurological dysfunctions and crime.

6. Explain the role of genes in predicting criminal behavior.

7. Explain human development, abnormal behavior, and crime from the psychodynamic perspective.

8. Describe the way behaviorists use conceptions of social learning and behavior modeling perspectives to understand criminal behavior.

9. Discuss the ways cognitive theorists analyze human perception and how it affects behavior.

10. Explain the ways psychological attributes such as personality and intelligence affect criminal behavior.

11. Discuss the social policy implications of biological and psychological treatment in criminal justice.

KEY TERMS AND CONCEPTS

Trait theories
Somatype
Mesomorph
Endomorph
Ectomorph
Sociobiology
Equipotentiality
Biophobia
Biochemical
Hypoglycemia
Testosterone
Androgens
Premenstrual syndrome
Neuro and Cerebral allergies
Environmental contaminants
Electroencephalograph
Minimal brain dysfunction

Attention deficit disorder
Neurotransmitters
Arousal theory
Monozygotic twins
Dizygotic twins
R/k selection theory
Cheater theory
Theory of imitation
Psychodynamic perspective
Oedipus complex
Electra complex
Psychosis
Neuroses
Schizophrenics
Identity crisis
Social learning theory

Cognitive theory
Moral and intellectual
      development theory
Sociopathy
Psychopathy
Antisocial personality
Nature theory
Nurture theory
Reciprocal altruism
Estrogen
Progesterone
Repression
Inferiority complex
Latent delinquency
Neuroticism

48

NAMES TO KNOW

Cesare Lombroso	Avshalom Caspi	David Lykken
Raffaele Garofalo	Charles Goring	Ogloff and Wong
Enrico Ferri	Gabriel Tarde	Lawrence Cohen
Richard Dugdale	Sigmund Freud	Bryan Vila
Arthur Estabrook	Alfred Adler	R. Starke Hathaway
William Sheldon	Erik Erikson	J. Charnley McKinley
Edmund O. Wilson	August Aichorn	Elio Monachesi
Stephen Schoenthaler	Albert Bandura	Karl Schuessler
D. Hill	David Phillips	Donald Cressey
W. Sargent	Garland White	Gordon Waldo
James Q. Wilson	Janet Katz	Simon Dinitz
Ellis and Coontz	Kathryn Scarborough	David Tennenbaum
Katharina Dalton	Wilhelm Wundt	Henry Goddard
Diana Fishbein	Edward Titchener	William Healy
Deborah Denno	William James	Augusta Bronner
Herbert Needleman	Jean Piaget	John Slawson
Terrie Moffit	Lawrence Kohlberg	Edwin Sutherland
Phil Silva	James Sorrell	Travis Hirschi
Eugene Maguin	Richard Rosner	Michael Hindelang
Lee Ellis	Bruce Link	Magda Stouthamer-Loeber
Karl Christiansen	Ellen Steury	Richard Hernnstein
David Rowe	Sheldon Glueck	Lorne Yeudall
D. Wayne Osgood	Eleanor Glueck	Hakan Stattin
Barry Hutchings	Hans Eysenck	Ingrid Klackenberg-Larsson
Sarnoff Mednick	Hervey Cleckley	Charles Murray
Byron Roth	Donald Lynam	

FILL-IN REVIEW

1. Biological explanations of criminal behavior first became popular during the middle part of the eighteenth century with the introduction of _____---the use of the scientific method and empirical analysis to study behavior.

2. Lombroso's identification of primitive _____ anomalies were based on what he believed was sound empirical research.

3. _____ differs from earlier theories of behavior in that it stresses that biological and genetic conditions affect the perception and learning of social behaviors, which in turn are linked to existing environmental structures.

4. Even when people come to the aid of others (_____ altruism), they are motivated by the belief that their actions will be reciprocated and that their gene survival capability will be enhanced.

5. Developed over the course of human history, _____ are inherited, natural and unlearned dispositions which activate specific behavior patterns that are designed to reach certain goals.

6. Some theorists believe that _____ factors, such as those produced by diet, environmental conditions, and allergies, control and influence violent behavior.

7. If people with normal needs do not receive the appropriate nutrition, they will suffer from _____ deficiency.

8. _____ occurs when glucose (sugar) in the blood falls below levels necessary for normal and efficient brain functioning.

9. _____, the principal male steroid hormone, controls secondary sex characteristics such as facial hair and voice timbre.

10. The female hormones estrogen and _____ have been administered to sex offenders in order to decrease their sexual potency.

11. _____ allergies cause an excessive reaction of the brain, whereas neuroallergies affect the nervous system.

12. An important measure of neurophysiological functioning is the _____.

13. _____ _____ dysfunction (MBD) has been defined as abruptly appearing, maladaptive behavior that interrupts the lifestyle and life flow of an individual.

14. Some psychologists view antisocial behavior from a _____ perspective--their focus is on early childhood experience and its effect on personality.

15. If conflicts are encountered during any of the psychosexual stages of development, a person can become _____ at that point.

16. People who experience feelings of mental anguish and are afraid that they are losing control of their personalities are said to be suffering from a form of _____ and are referred to as _____.

17. Erik Erikson (1902-1984) identified the _____ crisis--a period of serious personal questioning people undertake in an effort to determine their own values and sense of direction.

18. _____ learning theorists, most notably Albert Bandura, argue that people are not actually born with the ability to act violently but that they learn to be aggressive through their life experiences.

19. Psychologists from the _____ school focus on mental processes and the way people perceive and mentally represent the world around them, how they solve problems and how they perceive their environment.

20. _____ psychology stresses self-awareness and "getting in touch with feelings."

21. _____ can be defined as the reasonably stable patterns of behavior, including thoughts and emotions, that distinguish one person from another.

22. _____ are impulsive individuals who lack the ability to examine their own motives and behavior

50

23. _____ exhibit a low level of guilt and anxiety and persistently violate the rights of others.

24. _____ theory argues that intelligence is largely determined genetically, that ancestry determines IQ, and that low intelligence as demonstrated by low IQ is linked to behavior, including criminal behavior.

TRUE/FALSE

1. Biological and psychological theorists are not overly concerned with the legal definition of crime.

2. The work of Lombroso is regarded today as a significant piece of research.

3. Biosocial theorists assume that all humans are born with equal potential to learn and achieve (equipotentiality).

4. If people have genetic conditions that cause greater-than-normal needs for certain chemicals and minerals, they are said to suffer from nutritional vacancy.

5. The relationship between cerebral allergy dysfunction and crime first received a great deal of attention in 1968 when Charles Whitman barricaded himself in a tower at the University of Texas and proceeded to kill fourteen people.

6. Research efforts have linked abnormal EEG recordings to antisocial behavior in children.

7. Research has shown that although learning-disabled children violate the law at a higher rate than non-learning-disabled children, they are underrepresented in official arrest and juvenile court statistics.

8. Research by Terrie Moffitt and Phil Silva suggests that youths who suffer both ADD and MBD and who also grow up in a dysfunctional family are the ones most vulnerable to chronic and persistent delinquency.

9. Early research on individual families such as the Jukes and Kallikaks is taken seriously today.

10. When it was disclosed that Richard Speck actually had an extra Y chromosome interest in the XYY materialized.

11. Over the history of the human species aggressive males have had the greatest impact on the gene pool.

12. Part of the unconscious contains feelings about sex and hostility, which people keep below the surface of consciousness by a process called repression.

13. The id develops as a result of incorporating within the personality the moral standards and values of parents, community, and significant others.

14. Freud spent much time theorizing about crime.

15. Offenders classified as neurotics are driven by an unconscious desire to be punished for prior sins, either real or imaginary: they may violate the law to gain attention or punish parents.

16. The psychoanalyst whose work is most closely associated with criminality is Albert Bandura.

17. Behaviorists maintain that crimes, especially violent acts, are learned responses to life situations and do not necessarily represent abnormal or morally immature responses.

18. Social learning theorists view violence as something learned through a process called behavior modeling.

19. David Phillips found the homicide rate decreases marginally immediately after a heavyweight championship prize fight.

20. There have been numerous anecdotal cases of violence linked to TV and films.

21. Psychologists believe that media violence alone does cause violent behavior.

22. The moral and intellectual development branch of cognitive psychology is perhaps the most important for criminological theory.

23. Information processing has been used to explain the occurrence of date rape.

24. Three surveys of the literature on personality testing found strong evidence that personality traits could positively predict criminal involvement.

25. Early criminologists believed that low intelligence was a major cause of crime and delinquency.

MULTIPLE CHOICE

1. Biological explanations of crime fell out of favor in the:
   a. late eighteenth century
   b. early nineteenth century
   c. late nineteenth century
   d. early twentieth century
   e. late twentieth century

2. Sociobiologists view the _____ as the ultimate unit of life which controls all human destiny.
   a. brain
   b. gene
   c. androgen
   d. socio-interaction

3. Dan White, the killer of San Francisco Mayor George Moscone used the _____ defense which resulted in a jury finding him guilty of the lesser offense of diminished capacity manslaughter.
    a. instinctual
    b. vitamin
    c. cerebral
    d. twinky
    e. MBD

4. An important finding of Schoenthaler's study of the relationship between decreased sugar in the diet and institutional behavior:
    a. significant reduction in disciplinary actions
    b. significant increase in disciplinary actions
    c. an insignificant reduction in disciplinary actions
    d. an insignificant increase in disciplinary actions
    e. no noticeable difference in disciplinary actions

5. According to Ellis and Coontz, one of the physical reactions produced by hormones which influence violence is:
    a. a heightening of average resting arousal under normal environmental conditions
    b. a heightening of seizuring thresholds in and around the limbic system
    c. a rightward shift in neocortical functioning
    d. none of the above ("a" thru "c")

6. Which of the following is true about genetic influences:
    a. research on deviant families such as the Jukes and Kallikaks is taken seriously today
    b. recent evidence shows that animals cannot be bred to have passive-aggressive behavior traits
    c. John Hinckley was found to have an abnormal XYY chromosomal structure
    d. all of the above ("a" thru "c") is true
    e. none of the above ("a" thru "c") is true

7. Which of the following is true about adoption studies:
    a. Hutchings and Mednick found that the criminality of the biological father was a weak predictor of the child's criminal behavior
    b. Hutchings and Mednick found that the criminality of the adoptive father was a weak predictor of the child's criminal behavior
    c. when both the biological and adoptive father were criminal, the probability that the youth would engage in criminal behavior was still a weak predictor of the child's criminal behavior
    d. all of the above is true ("a" thru "c")
    e. none of the above is true ("a" thru "c")

8. Biological theory is challenged by critics because it:
    a. seems less concerned with the effect of a crime-producing social environment
    b. ignores the blue-collar crime of the middle- and lower-classes
    c. seems to give too much weight to geographic and temporal patterns
    d. all of the above challenged biological theory ("a" thru "c")
    e. none of the above challenged biological theory ("a" thru "c")

9. Which of the following is <u>true</u> about biosocial theory:
   a. the most significant strength of the approach has been the abundance of valid empirical theory
   b. a great deal of biosocial research is conducted with samples of adjudicated offenders who have been placed in clinical treatment settings
   c. the methodology has been well designed
   d. the use of statistical techniques has been limited to trivariate analysis

10. The forerunner of modern-day learning theorists:
    a. Gabriel Tarde
    b. Henry Maudsley
    c. Charles Goring
    d. all of the above are forerunners of modern-day theorists ("a" thru "c")
    e. none of the above are forerunners of modern-day theorists ("a" thru "c")

11. _____ theorists analyze human perception and how it affects behavior.
    a. Psychoanalytic
    b. Behavioral
    c. Cognitive
    d. Psychodramatic
    e. Sociopathic

12. The _____ mind contains elements of experiences that are out of awareness but can be brought back to consciousness at any time--memories, experiences.
    a. unconscious
    b. subconscious
    c. endoconscious
    d. preconscious

13. The id follows the _____ principle.
    a. reality
    b. pleasure
    c. moral
    d. natural

14. Freud postulates that the most basic human drive, or instinct, present at birth is _____, the instinct to preserve and create life.
    a. Zeus
    b. Miranda
    c. Poseidon
    d. Eros
    e. Electra

15. <u>Latency</u> begins at age _____; during this period, feelings of sexuality are repressed until the <u>genital stage</u> begins at puberty.
    a. two
    b. four
    c. six
    d. eight
    e. ten

16. Those people who have lost total control and who are dominated by their id are known as
    _____.
    a. psychotics
    b. neurotics
    c. oedipus
    d. fixated

17. August Aichorn concluded that societal stress, though damaging, could not alone result in a life of crime unless a predisposition existed that prepared youths psychologically for antisocial acts. Aichorn labeled this state _____ delinquency.
    a. preconscious
    b. repressed
    c. primitive
    d. latent

18. Social learning theorists have suggested that violence and aggression are produced by:
    a. an event that heightens arousal
    b. aggressive skills
    c. expected positive outcomes
    d. none of the above ("a" thru "c")
    e. all of the above ("a" thru "c")

19. A sub-discipline within the cognitive perspective:
    a. rational development branch
    b. information processing branch
    c. normative-reeducative branch
    d. none of the above ("a" thru "c")

20. Lawrence Kohlberg's sixth stage of development is:
    a. right is taking responsibility for oneself
    b. right is being good in the sense of having food motives
    c. right is maintaining the rules of a society and serving the welfare
    d. right is based on recognized individual rights within a society
    e. right is an assumed obligation to principles applying to all humankind

21. A type of standardized personality test:
    a. projective techniques
    b. latent methods
    c. California Inkblot Index
    d. Minnesota Secondary Registers

22. After re-examining existing research data, Hirschi and Hindelang concluded that:
    a. social class is more important than race or IQ for predicting criminal and delinquent involvement
    b. race is more important than social class or IQ for predicting criminal and delinquent involvement
    c. IQ is more important than race and social class for predicting criminal and delinquent involvement
    d. age is more important than social class, race, or IQ for predicting criminal and delinquent involvement

23. _____ are tall and thin and less social and more intellectual than the other types of distinct physiques.
   a.   Ectomorphs
   b.   Schizothymes
   c.   Mesomorphs
   d.   Endomorphs
   d.   Towermorphs

MATCHING

____   1.   Sociobiology   A.   Androgens
____   2.   "Biometric method"   B.   Moral standards
____   3.   Male sex hormones   C.   Alfred Adler
____   4.   Neurophysiology   D.   Lack of insight
____   5.   Diet   E.   Study of brain activity
____   6.   Psychoanalytic psychology   F.   Practicality & convention
____   7.   Superego   G.   Genes
____   8.   Ego   H.   MMPI
____   9.   Schizophrenia   I.   Lawrence Kohlberg
____   10. Inferiority complex   J.   Charles Goring
____   11. Stages of moral development   K.   Sigmund Freud
____   12. Psychological testing   L.   Twinky defense

ESSAY QUESTIONS

1.   What are the problems with Lombroso's methodology?

2.   From a sociobiologist framework, identify and describe the factors which are important in understanding behavior.

3.   What are the significant dimensions of biosocial theory?

4.   What is the relationship between vitamin deficiency/dependency and antisocial behavior?

5.   Describe the findings of research on hormones and crime.

6.   Give an example of the relationship between neurological dysfunction and crime.

7.   What have the findings of EEG recordings suggested about the origins of antisocial behavior?

8.   Describe the relationship between ADD and MBD dysfunctions and delinquent careers.

9.   What is the XYY controversy?

10. What do twin studies tell us about the genetic origins of crime?

11. What are some typical criticisms of the biosocial perspective?

12. How does Freudian theory characterize the mind, personality, and developmental stages?

13.   Describe the various views of psychoanalysts toward the relationship between abnormal mental states and criminality. Do research studies support psychoanalytical perspectives? Explain.

14.   How do behavioralists explain human actions? What are the premises of the social learning approach toward the origins of violence?

15.   Does broadcast violence cause aggressive behavior in viewers? Explain.

16.   Compare and contrast the approaches within the cognitive school called moral development and information processing.

17.   List Kohlberg's stages of moral development. What are the implications of moral development theory to understanding criminal behavior?

18.   What is the relationship between personality and criminality? How important is the concept of psychopaths to understanding criminal behavior?

19.   Describe the findings of research on personality.

20.   Define the nature of the debate over the relationship between intelligence and crime. What are the results of research on IQ and criminality?

21.   What are the social policy implications of both biologically oriented therapy and psychological treatment?

CHAPTER SIX ANSWER SECTION

FILL-IN REVIEW

1. positivism
2. atavistic
3. Sociobiology
4. reciprocal
5. instincts
6. biochemical
7. vitamin
8. Hypoglycemia
9. Testosterone
10. progesterone
11. Cerebral
12. electroencephalograph
13. Minimal brain
14. psychoanalytic
15. fixated
16. neuroses; neurotics
17. identity
18. Social
19. cognitive
20. Humanistic
21. Personality
22. Extraverts
23. Psychopaths
24. Nature

TRUE/FALSE

1. T
2. F
3. F
4. F
5. F
6. T
7. F
8. T
9. F
10. F
11. T
12. T
13. F
14. F
15. T
16. F
17. T
18. T
19. F
20. T
21. F
22. T
23. T
24. F
25. T

MULTIPLE CHOICE

1. d
2. b
3. d
4. a
5. c
6. e
7. e
8. a
9. b
10. a
11. c
12. d
13. b
14. d
15. c
16. a
17. d
18. e
19. b
20. e
21. a
22. c
23. a

MATCHING

1. G
2. J
3. A
4. E
5. L
6. K
7. B
8. F
9. D
10. C
11. I
12. H

7 *Social Structure Theories*

LEARNING OBJECTIVES

1. Identify the reasons for the predominant role of sociology in modern criminology.

2. Explain how the structure of American society promotes criminal behavior.

3. Define the social structure perspective.

4. Describe social disorganization theory, especially as developed by Shaw and McKay. Identify the contributions of Shaw and McKay.

5. Describe the views of strain theorists, especially as developed in Robert Merton's theory of anomie and Judith and Peter Blau's approach to relative deprivation theory.

6. Compare and contrast Sellin's conduct norms to Miller's focal concern theory.

7. Explain the meaning and worth of Albert Cohen's theory of delinquent subcultures.

8. Explain Cloward and Ohlin's theory of differential opportunity.

9. Describe the development and the importance of the gang through time.

10. Discuss the relationship between social structure theory and social policy.

KEY TERMS AND CONCEPTS

Chicago school	Transitional neighborhoods	Affluent families
Stratified	Value conflict	General strain theory
Poverty line	Social ecology	Negative affective states
Lower-class culture	Incivilities	Cultural deviance
Racial disparity	Siege mentality	Culture conflict
Culture of poverty	Gentrification	Conduct norms
Underclass	Concentration effect	Focal concerns
At-risk	Social controls	Status frustration
Truly disadvantaged	Social altruism	Middle-class measuring rods
Undeserving poor	Anomie	Short-run hedonism
Social structure theory	Normlessness	Group autonomy
Social disorganization	Social adaptation	Reaction formation
Strain theory	Income inequality	Differential opportunity
Cultural deviance theory	Inegalitarian societies	Chicago area project
Subculture	Relative deprivation	Mobilization for youth
Cultural transmission	Social injustice	Social embeddedness

NAMES TO KNOW

Robert Ezra Park	Solomon Kobrin	Robert Agnew
Ernest W. Burgess	Janet Heitgerd	Paul Mazerolle
Louis Wirth	Carolyn Block	Alex Piquero
Harvey Zorbaugh	Richard Block	Helene Raskin White
Frederick Thrasher	Mitchell Chamlin	John Hoffman
Oscar Lewis	John Cochran	S. Susan Su
Gunnar Myrdal	Emile Durkheim	Lisa Broidy
William Julius Wilson	Robert Merton	Robbin Ogle
Henry McKay	Steven Messner	Thorsten Sellin
Clifford R. Shaw	Richard Rosenfeld	Walter Miller
Bernard Lander	John Braithwaite	Albert Cohen
David Bordua	Judith Blau	Richard Cloward
Roland Chilton	Peter Blau	Lloyd Ohlin
G. David Curry	Gary LaFree	Cheryl Maxson
Irving Spergel	Kriss Drass	Malcolm Klein
Robert Bursik	Nikos Passas	Robert Sampson
Harold Grasmick	Roy Austin	John Hagan
Leo Scheurman	Chris Hebert	

FILL-IN REVIEW

1.   Park and Burgess studied the social ecology of Chicago and found that some neighborhoods form _____ areas of wealth and affluence, while others suffered poverty and disintegration.

2.   Social _____ are segments of the population whose members have a relatively similar share of desirable things and who share attitudes, values, norms, and an identifiable lifestyle.

3.   Oscar Lewis argued that the lifestyle of slums produce a culture of _____ passed from one generation to the next.

4.   Since the truly _____ rarely come into contact with the actual source of their oppression, they direct their anger and aggression at those with whom they are in close and intimate contact.

5.   As a group _____ _____ theories suggest that forces operating in the lower-class areas of the environment push many of their residents into criminal behavior patterns.

6.   Social _____ theory focuses on conditions in the urban environment that impact on crime.

7.   _____ _____ theory, the third variation of structural theory, combines elements of both strain and social disorganization. According to this view, because of strain and social isolation, a unique lower-class culture develops in disorganized neighborhoods.

8.   Subcultural values are handed down from one generation to the next in a process called cultural _____ .

9.   Researchers have found that urban areas may undergo _____, which begin with the building of residential dwellings, followed by a period of decline with marked decreases in socio-economic status and increase in population density.

10.   The best known strain theory is Robert Merton's theory of _____.

11.   Merton argues that each person has his or her own concept of the _____ of society and the _____ at his or her disposal to attain them.

12.   _____ occurs when an individual accepts the goals of society but rejects or is incapable of using legitimate means to attain them.

13.   _____ results when goals are lowered in importance and means are at the same time rigidly adhered to.

14.   _____ entails a rejection of both the goals and the means of society.

15.   Messner and Rosenfeld agree with Merton's view that the success goal is pervasive in American culture. They refer to this as the American _____, a term which they employ as both a goal and a process.

16.   If income inequality causes strain, then it stands to reason that crime rates will be highest in areas where the affluent and indigent live in close proximity to one another. This is referred to as _____ deprivation.

17.   Judith and Peter Blau maintain that a sense of social _____ directly related to inequality in communities in which the poor and wealthy live in close proximity to one another leads to a state of disorganization and anger.

18.   Sellin argues that ethnic and racial minorities maintain their own set of _____ norms-- rules governing the day-to-day living conditions within their subcultures.

19.   Because social conditions make them incapable of achieving success legitimately, lower-class youths experience a form of culture conflict that Albert Cohen labels _____ frustration.

20.   According to Albert Cohen, the college boy actively strives to be successful by middle-class standards rather than scorning middle-class _____ _____.

21.   Although Albert Cohen believes _____ hedonism is a characteristic of lower-class culture as a whole, he finds it especially applicable to delinquent groups. Delinquents live for today and let "tomorrow take care of itself."

22.   The centerpiece of the Cloward and Ohlin theory is the concept of _____ opportunity.

TRUE/FALSE

1.   Ecological differences in the crime rate can be explained by chemical or chromosome abnormality.

2.   Embeddedness in a deviant lifestyle is contrasted with the establishment of roots in a conventional one: youths who get early work experience, who make contacts and learn the ropes of the job market establish the groundwork for a successful career.

3.   The lower class consists of an estimated 65.1 million Americans who live in poverty.

4.   Black poverty has actually increased in the South.

5.   Social disorganization theory views crime-ridden neighborhoods as ones in which residents are trying to leave at the earliest opportunity.

6.   Shaw and McKay found that even though crime rates changed, the highest rates were always in zones VI and VII.

7.   Shaw and McKay believed that neighborhood disintegration and slum conditions are the primary causes of criminal behavior.

8.   There is strong evidence that links unemployment to high crime rates.

9.   Unemployment seems to have the greatest influence on violent assaultive crimes and the least on property crimes.

10.   Recent studies recognize that change and not stability is the hallmark of inner city areas.

11.   Strain theorists view crime as a direct result of the frustration and anger people experience over their inability to achieve the social and financial success they desire.

12.   If a society becomes anomic, it can no longer establish and maintain control over its population's wants and desires.

13.   Merton explains why people differ in their choice of criminal behavior.

14.   Agnew found that the desire for unlimited goals was related to personal frustration and criminality in all elements of the class structure.

15.   Research shows that crime rates begin to increase when contiguous neighborhoods become polarized by class.

16.   People living in urban ghettos suffer higher rates of unemployment, are more dependent on welfare and more likely to live in single-parent households than equally indigent people who reside in more affluent areas.

17.   The central premise of Albert Cohen's theory was that delinquent behavior of middle-class youths is actually a protest against the norms and values of the lower-class culture in the U.S.

18.   Retreatists are double failures, unable to gain success through legitimate means and unwilling to do so through illegal ones.

19.   Cloward and Ohlin portray delinquent youths as having values in opposition to middle-class culture.

20.   National surveys find that people in the lowest income brackets want tougher drug laws, more police protection, and greater control over criminal offenders.

MULTIPLE CHOICE

1.   An important social change has been the rapid increase in _____ and its influence on the social system.
      a.   religion
      b.   technology
      c.   leisure
      d.   population
      e.   longevity

2.   People in the United States live in a _____ society.
      a.   hierarchical
      b.   disorganized
      c.   concentrated
      d.   stratified

3.   One branch within the social structure perspective:
      a.   social imbalance
      b.   sociological traits
      c.   social control
      d.   social disorganization

4.   _____ theory holds that crime is a function of the conflict between the goals and desires lower class people strive for and what they can realistically hope to achieve in American society.
      a.   Robertian
      b.   Strain
      c.   Radical
      d.   Anomie
      e.   Parallel

5.   Cultural deviance theory suggests that because of strain and social isolation, independent _____ develop in disorganized neighborhoods. These _____ maintain a unique set of values and beliefs that are in conflict with conventional social norms.
      a.   groups
      b.   families
      c.   subcultures
      d.   collectives
      e.   institutions

6.   Shaw and McKay noted that distinct ecological areas had developed in Chicago, comprising a series of _____ concentric circles, or zones, and that there were stable and significant differences in inter-zone crime rates.
      a.   three
      b.   five
      c.   seven
      d.   nine
      e.   eleven

7.   Of the five individual modes of adaptation developed by Merton, _____ is most closely associated with criminal behavior.
    a.   conformity
    b.   innovation
    c.   ritualism
    d.   retreatism
    e.   rebellion

8.   Included in this category of _____ are "psychotics, psychoneurotics, pariahs, outcasts, vagrants, vagabonds, tramps, and chronic drunkards."
    a.   conformity
    b.   innovation
    c.   ritualism
    d.   retreatism
    e.   rebellion

9.   This adaptation involves the substitution of alternative sets of goals and means for the accepted ones of society.
    a.   conformity
    b.   innovation
    c.   ritualism
    d.   retreatism
    e.   rebellion

10.   Middle-class culture stresses:
    a.   immediate gratification
    b.   excitement
    c.   being cautious
    d.   risk taking
    e.   fearlessness

11.   According to Sellin _____ conflict occurs when the rules expressed in the criminal law clash with the demands of group conduct norms.
    a.   family
    b.   neighborhood
    c.   community
    d.   culture
    e.   societal

12.   According to Walter Miller, _____ to the lower-class citizen, means knowing essential survival techniques like gambling, conning, and outfoxing one's opponent.
    a.   trouble
    b.   toughness
    c.   smartness
    d.   excitement
    e.   fate

13.   According to Albert Cohen, the _____ boy hangs out in the neighborhood, engages in gambling, and is truant.
      a.   choir
      b.   corner
      c.   cultured
      d.   college
      e.   delinquent

14.   Symptoms of _____ formation include overly intense responses that seem disproportionate to the stimuli that trigger them.
      a.   reaction
      b.   cohesive
      c.   autonomous
      d.   hedonistic
      e.   differential

15.   Disorganized neighborhoods suffer social and physical _____ --- rowdy youth, trash and litter, graffiti, abandoned storefronts, burned-out buildings, littered lots, strangers, drunks, vagabonds, loiterers, prostitutes, noise, congestion, dirt, and stench.
      a.   disecology
      b.   deconstructionism
      c.   instability
      d.   misterioration
      e.   incivilities

16.   Cloward and Ohlin maintain that _____ gangs develop in communities unable to provide legitimate nor illegitimate opportunities.
      a.   malefactor
      b.   conflict
      c.   sanctuary
      d.   drug
      e.   semiprofessional theft

17.   According to Cloward and Ohlin, during this "apprenticeship stage" older, more experienced members of the _____ subculture hold tight reins on youthful "trainees," limiting activities that might jeopardize the gang's profits (for example, engaging in non-functional, irrational violence).
      a.   criminal
      b.   structured
      c.   corporate
      d.   organizational
      e.   middle-class

18.   Personal status in the _____ subculture is derived from peer approval, a subculture in which each member wants to be both the "coolest" guy in his group and detached from relationship with the conventional world.
      a.   outlaw
      b.   harmonious
      c.   retreatist
      d.   parent male
      e.   middle-class

19. Of the 150 cities in the United States with populations of more than 100,000, _____ percent had experienced gang migration from larger cities.
    a. 29
    b. 44
    c. 67
    d. 82

20. The National Assessment of Gang Activity, a survey, found that _____ percent of the nation's 79 largest cities report the presence of youth gangs involved in criminal activity.
    a. 99
    b. 91
    c. 85
    d. 74

21. Why has gang activity increased? One compelling reason why gang activity and membership has soared in the past decade is:
    a. poverty
    b. drugs
    c. competition
    d. better organization
    e. stronger leadership

MATCHING

____	1.	Robert Ezra Park	A.	Social embeddedness
____	2.	Culture of poverty	B.	Differential opportunity
____	3.	Shaw and McKay	C.	College fraternities
____	4.	John Hagan	D.	Organizing existing community structure
____	5.	Renewal housing stage	E.	Chicago sociologist
____	6.	Ritualism	F.	Fate
____	7.	Retreatism	G.	War on Poverty
____	8.	Focal concern	H.	Apathy, cynicism, mistrust
____	9.	Albert Cohen	I.	Gentrification
____	10.	Cloward and Ohlin	J.	"In the society but not of it"
____	11.	Chicago Area Project	K.	Middle-class measuring rods
____	12.	Mobilization for Youth	L.	Five concentric circles

ESSAY QUESTIONS

1. Why has sociology remained the predominant approach of American criminologists during the twentieth century?

2. What are the problems of lower-class culture?

3. What are the distinct problems of African-Americans?

4. Define the perspective of social structure theories.

5. Identify and compare the three overlapping branches within the social structure perspective.

6.   Describe the work of Shaw and McKay. In what ways is their work important? How has their work been criticized?

7.   Describe the social disorganization findings in other cultures.

8.   How is social disorganization related to employment opportunities and to community fear?

9.   Define Merton's theory of anomie. Compare and contrast the five types of individual modes of adaptation.

10.   Describe the theory of relative deprivation. What are the findings of research on this theory?

11.   Under what conditions will culture conflict occur?

12.   Identify and describe the focal concerns of the lower class.

13.   Describe Cohen's theory of delinquent subcultures. What are the causes of delinquency? Define the meaning and importance of the concepts of "middle-class measuring rods," "short-run hedonism," and "reaction formation."

14.   Evaluate Cohen's work.

15.   Define Cloward and Ohlin's theory of differential opportunity. Identify and describe their three types of collective responses to blocked legitimate opportunities. What are the findings of research on their theory?

16.   What is a delinquent gang? Trace the development of gangs through time. Why has gang activity increased in recent years?

17.   How has social structural theory influenced social policy?

CHAPTER SEVEN ANSWER SECTION

FILL-IN REVIEW

1.	natural		12.	Innovation
2.	classes		13.	Ritualism
3.	poverty		14.	Retreatism
4.	disadvantaged		15.	Dream
5.	social structure		16.	relative
6.	disorganization		17.	injustice
7.	Cultural deviance		18.	conduct
8.	transmission		19.	status
9.	lifecycles		20.	measuring rods
10.	anomie		21.	short-run
11.	goals; means		22.	differential

TRUE/FALSE

1.	F	11.	T
2.	T	12.	T
3.	F	13.	F
4.	F	14.	T
5.	T	15.	T
6.	F	16.	T
7.	T	17.	F
8.	F	18.	T
9.	F	19.	F
10.	T	20.	T

MULTIPLE CHOICE

1.	b	12.	c
2.	d	13.	b
3.	d	14.	a
4.	b	15.	e
5.	c	16.	b
6.	b	17.	a
7.	b	18.	c
8.	d	19.	d
9.	e	20.	b
10.	c	21.	b
11.	d		

MATCHING

1.	E
2.	H
3.	L
4.	A
5.	I
6.	C
7.	J
8.	F
9.	K
10.	B
11.	D
12.	G

8 Social Process Theories

LEARNING OBJECTIVES

1. Describe the role of family, peer group, and school in the development of criminal careers.

2. Explain the principles underpinning differential association theory.

3. Explain Akers's differential reinforcement theory.

4. Describe neutralization theory and the techniques that are used by juveniles.

5. Evaluate the research that has tested the three prominent forms of social learning theory.

6. Define the control theory perspective.

7. Explain the social control theory developed by Travis Hirschi.

8. Explain and evaluate the labeling theory perspective on crime and deviance.

9. Explain the ways criminological theories have been integrated in an attempt to develop comprehensive models of crime and delinquency.

10. Identify the strengths and weaknesses of the social process approach.

11. Describe the role of social process theory in social policy.

KEY TERMS AND CONCEPTS

Social-psychological Processes
Socialization
Broken home
Social learning theory
Differential association theory
Differential reinforcement theory
Association
Imitation
Neutralization theory
Drift

Subterranean value
social control theory
Self-control
Self-esteem
Containment theory
Social bond
Labeling theory
differential enforcement
Stigma
Dramatization of evil

Moral entrepeneurs
Social distance
Secondary deviance
Head start
Cliques
Commitment to conformity
Symbolic interaction
Social deviant
Reflective role-taking
Reflected appraisal

69

NAMES TO KNOW

Charles Tittle	David Matza	Randy LaGrange
Robert Meier	Gresham Sykes	Helene Raskin White
James Q. Wilson	Michael Hindelang	Charles Horton Cooley
Richard Herrnstein	Robert Agnew	George Herbert Mead
John Laub	Mark Pogrebin	Herbert Blumer
Robert Sampson	Scott Briar	Kai Erickson
Travis Hirschi	Irving Piliavin	Edwin Schur
Rodney Stark	Walter Reckless	Frank Tannenbaum
T. David Evans	Teresa LaGrange	Edwin Lemert
Edwin H. Sutherland	Robert Silverman	Howard Kaplan
Donald Cressey	Velmer Burton	Karen Heimer
James Short	Kimberly Kempf-Leonard	Ross Matsueda
Albert Reiss	Scott Decker	Carl Pope
A. Lewis Rhodes	Gary Jensen	William Feyerheim
Mark Warr	David Brownfield	Leslie Margolin
Kenneth Tunnell	Leslie Samuelson	Lawrence Sherman
Yuet-Wah Cheung	Timothy Hartnagel	Douglas Smith
Agnes M. C. Ng	Harvey Krahn	Robert Brame
Ronald Akers	Marvin Krohn	Charles Wellford
Craig Reinerman	James Massey	Raymond Paternoster
Jeffrey Fagan	Jill Leslie Rosenbaum	Leeann Iovanni
Robert Burgess	James Lasley	

FILL-IN REVIEW

1. Social process theories hold that criminality is a function of individual _____ and the social-psychological interactions people have with the various organizations, institutions, and processes of society.

2. As they go through adolescence, children form _____, small groups of friends who share activities and confidences.

3. _____ exert a powerful influence on youth and pressure them to conform to group values.

4. Sykes and Matza suggest that juveniles develop a distinct set of justifications for their law-violating behavior. These neutralization techniques allow youths to temporarily move away from the rules of the normative society and participate in _____ behaviors.

5. _____ _____ theory maintains that everyone has the potential to become a criminal but that most people are controlled by their bond to society.

6. _____ _____ (1883-1950), often considered the preeminent U.S. criminologist, crafted the theory of differential association.

7. Differential _____ theory (also called social learning theory) is an attempt to explain crime as a type of learned behavior.

8.   According to Akers, people learn social behavior by _____ conditioning, behavior controlled by stimuli that follow the behavior.

9.   Matza maintains that the movement from one extreme of behavior to another (e.g., total freedom to total restraint) is a process which he calls _____.

10.   Sykes and Matza conclude that delinquency is the result of the _____ of accepted social values through the learning of a standard set of techniques which allow youths to counteract the moral dilemmas posed by illegal behavior.

11.   Walter Reckless called an individual's ability to resist criminal inducements _____, the most important of which are a positive self image and "ego strength."

12.   Hirschi argues that people who live in the same social setting often share common moral _____; they may adhere to such values as sharing, sensitivity to the rights of others, and admiration for the legal code.

13.   Adults who have been given official _____ such as "criminal" or "addict" may find their eligibility for employment severely restricted.

14.   "_____ is not a property inherent in certain forms of behavior," argues sociologist Kai Erickson, "it is a property conferred upon those forms by the audience which directly or indirectly witnesses them."

15.   If they are not really evil or bad, they may ask themselves, why is everyone making such a fuss about them, a process that Frank Tannenbaum referred to as the _____ of evil.

16.   According to Lemert, _____ deviance involves norms violations or crimes that have very little influence on the actor and can be quickly forgotten.

17.   If a devalued _____ is conferred by a significant other---teacher, police officer, elder, parent or valued peer---the negative label may cause permanent harm to their targets.

18.   Heimer and Matsueda found that reflected _____ as a rule-violator has a significant effect on delinquency: Kids who believe that their parents and friends consider them deviants and troublemakers are the ones most likely to engage in delinquency.

TRUE/FALSE

1.   According to social process theories, all people, regardless of their race, class or gender, have the potential to become delinquents or criminals.

2.   After many years of research, criminologists have found a clear-cut empirical relationship between social class and crime rates.

3.   Relatively few delinquent offenders living in deteriorated areas remain persistent, chronic offenders.

4.   John Laub and Robert Sampson have found evidence that the children of parents who engage in criminality and substance abuse are more likely to engage in law violating behavior than the offspring of conventional parents.

5.   Child abuse is most prevalent among families living in socially disorganized neighborhoods, explaining in part the association between poverty and violence.

6.   Sutherland's research on white-collar crime, professional theft, and intelligence led him to the notion that crime was a function of the inadequacy of people in the middle and upper classes.

7.   Cressey believed that criminal behavior is an inherent characteristic of born criminals.

8.   Sutherland believed that the desire to accumulate money or social status, personal frustration, or low self-concept are causes of crimes.

9.   Sutherland maintained that a person becomes delinquent when he or she perceives more favorable than unfavorable consequences to violating the law.

10. The principles of the theory of differential association readily fit empirical measurement.

11. Differential association provides a consistent explanation of all types of delinquent and criminal behavior.

12. Differential reinforcement theory suggests that behavior is weakened by negative stimuli (punishment) and loss of reward (negative punishment).

13. Akers found that kids who believed they would be rewarded for deviance by those they respect were the ones most likely to engage in deviant behavior.

14. A valid test of neutralization theory would have to be able to show that a person first drifted into delinquency and then neutralized his or her moral beliefs.

15. Empirical research indicates that an important association between self-image and delinquency may in fact exist.

16. Reckless's central premise is that people are "controlled" by their feelings towards themselves and others they are in contact with.

17. Hirschi assumes that not all individuals are potential law violators.

18. Hirschi views society as containing competing subcultures with unique value systems.

19. One of Hirschi's most significant contributions was his attempt to test the principal hypotheses of social control theory.

20. Research efforts have disputed Hirschi's view that delinquents are lone wolves whose only personal relationships are exploitive.

21. The weight of the existing empirical evidence is not supportive of control theory.

22. Sutherland did not specify what he meant by priority, but Cressey and others have interpreted the term to mean the age of children when they first encounter definitions of criminality.

23. In its purest form, labeling theory argues that crimes such as murder, rape, and assault are only bad or evil because people label them as such.

72

24.   A major premise of labeling theory is that the law is equally applied.

25.   Labeling theorists are especially concerned with explaining why people originally engage in acts that result in their being labeled.

26.   Primary deviance produces a deviance amplification effect.

27.   The evidence that the justice system is inherently unfair and biased is inconclusive.

28.   The majority of research studies support the belief that stigma-reducing programs have generally met with great success.

29.   While his research is generally supportive of DA, Warr discovered that recent rather than early friends had the greatest influence on criminality, a finding which contradicts DA's emphasis on the "priority" of criminal influences.

30.   There is little existing evidence that people learn the techniques that enable them to become criminals before they actually commit criminal acts.

MULTIPLE CHOICE

1.   Many criminologists question whether a person's place in the social structure _____ can control the onset of criminality. After all, the majority of people residing in the nation's most deteriorated urban areas are law-abiding citizens who hold conventional values and compensate for their lack of social standing and financial problems by hard work, frugal living, and an eye to the future.
       a.   motivationally
       b.   operationally
       c.   embarkation
       d.   alone

2.   Elements of socialization include:
       a.   family
       b.   peer group
       c.   school
       d.   agents of the criminal justice system
       e.   all of the above ("a" thru "d")

3.   Which of the following is one of the prominent forms of social learning theory:
       a.   differential nullification theory
       b.   differential labeling theory
       c.   differential control theory
       d.   differential reinforcement theory

4.   Which of the following is an idea that Sutherland would favor:
       a.   an individual becomes a law violator simply by living in a crimogenic environment
       b.   movies and television are principal parts of the learning of criminal behavior
       c.   criminal behavior is not similar to other learned behavior
       d.   reaction to social rules and laws is uniform across society
       e.   none of the above ("a" thru "d")

5. Which of the following is an idea that Sykes and Matza would favor:
   a. delinquents lack a sense of guilt over their illegal acts
   b. juvenile offenders rarely respect and admire honest, law-abiding persons
   c. delinquents draw a line between those whom they can victimize and those whom they cannot
   d. delinquents are immune to the demands of conformity
   e. none of the above ("a" thru "d")

6. Denial of responsibility refers to a belief that:
   a. criminal acts were accidents
   b. stealing is viewed as a form of borrowing
   c. the victim of crime "had it coming"
   d. the world is a corrupt place with a dog-eat-dog code
   e. the needs of the group take precedence over the rules of society

7. Control theorists argue that people obey the law because they:
   a. fear punishment
   b. have access to legitimate opportunities
   c. process information clearly
   d. have a commitment to conformity

8. Reckless focused on containments such as:
   a. a nuclear family
   b. excellent schools
   c. balanced diet
   d. positive self image

9. Reckless argues that external _____ are adverse living conditions that influence deviant behavior such as relative deprivation, poverty, unemployment, insecurity, etc.
   a. phylloxera
   b. pressures
   c. pulls
   d. pochard
   e. pushes

10. Hirschi argues that _____ refers to a person's sensitivity to and interest in others.
    a. belief
    b. commitment
    c. attachment
    d. involvement
    e. none of the above ("a" thru "d")

11. Hirschi maintains that _____ involves the time, energy, and effort expended in conventional lines of action.
    a. belief
    b. commitment
    c. attachment
    d. involvement
    e. none of the above ("a" thru "d")

12. Hirschi found in his research that:
   a. youths who were strongly attached to their parents were less likely to commit criminal acts
   b. delinquents and nondelinquents differ in their beliefs about society
   c. delinquent youths maintained strong relationships with people
   d. none of the above is a finding ("a" thru "c")
   e. all of the above are findings ("a" thru "c")

13. Those who oppose Hirschi's theory have found that control variables were better able to explain:
   a. female delinquency than male delinquency
   b. minor delinquency than more serious criminal acts
   c. friendship patterns of marginal delinquents than serious delinquents
   d. both "a" and "b" are findings in opposition

14. The most severe criticism of control theory has been leveled by sociologist Robert Agnew, who claims that Hirschi:
   a. should have focused on the relationship between self confidence and self-control
   b. miscalculated the direction of the relationship between criminality and weak social bonds
   c. developed an explanation for individual differences in the tendency to commit criminal acts that overemphasized the attachment to peers
   d. none of the above ("a" thru "c")

15. A process in which the past of the labeled person is reviewed and re-evaluated to fit his or her current outcast status is called _____ reading.
   a. degradation
   b. stigmatized
   c. retrospective
   d. regressive

16. _____ deviance occurs when a deviant event comes to the attention of significant others or social control agents who apply a negative label.
   a. Progressive
   b. Secondary
   c. Closet
   d. Meaningful

17. Labeling theory has been criticized for:
   a. its inability to specify conditions that must exist before an act or individual is labeled deviant
   b. its failure to explain differences in crime rates
   c. its failure to explain the onset of deviant behavior
   d. both "a" and "b"
   e. all of the above ("a" thru "c")

18. While it is true that criticisms of labeling theory has reduced its importance in the criminological literature, its utility as an explanation of crime and deviance should not be dismissed. It has special value as an explanation of:
   a. both control and cultural deviance theories
   b. schools as a front-line defense to a criminal career
   c. chronic offending
   d. the high crime rates found in lower-class area
   e. the positive influence of critical agents of the social order on criminal behavior

MATCHING

____	1.	Crowds	A.	Social control theory
____	2.	Edwin Sutherland	B.	"At times I think I am no good at all"
____	3.	Ronald Akers	C.	Author of Neutralization theory
____	4.	David Matza	D.	Family structure
____	5.	Travis Hirschi	E.	Residential treatment program
____	6.	Broken home	F.	Mutually shared activities
____	7.	Denial of injury	G.	Label-avoiding innovation
____	8.	Self-rejection	H.	Stealing is viewed as borrowing
____	9.	Highfields Project	I.	Differential association theory
____	10.	Restitution	J.	Containment theory
____	11.	Denial of victim	K.	"Had it coming"
____	12.	Walter Reckless	L.	Differential reinforcement theory

ESSAY QUESTIONS

1.   How do the elements of socialization such as the family, school, and peer group contribute to the development of a criminal career?

2.   Which youth are "at risk" in the United States?

3.   Define and explain the basic principles of differential association. Evaluate the findings of research on differential association.

4.   Define differential reinforcement theory. Describe Ronald Akers's characterization of the theory. Evaluate the findings of Akers's research.

5.   What are techniques of neutralization that juveniles develop for their law violating behavior?

6.   What are the problems that have been identified with the learning model?

7.   According to containment theory, what are the crime producing forces which a strong self image counteracted?

8.   Identify and describe Hirschi's social bond elements. What were the results of Hirschi's attempt to test the principal hypotheses of social control theory?

9.   Identify and describe the findings of research which support as well as undercut Hirschi's work.

10.   How does labeling theory explain criminal career formation?

11.   How do negative labels result in stigma?

12.   What are the differences between primary and secondary deviance?

13.   Describe the findings of research on labeling theory.

14.   What are the criticisms of labeling theory offered by Charles Wellford?

15.   How valuable are Head Start programs? Explain.

16.   Why is the work by Heimer and Matsueda important? Explain.

17.   How does Howard Kaplan's General Theory of Deviance draw upon labeling theory concepts?

18.   What are the strengths and weaknesses of social process theory?

19.   How have social process theories influenced social policy making?

CHAPTER EIGHT ANSWER SECTION

FILL-IN REVIEW

1.	socialization	10.	neutralization
2.	cliques	11.	containment
3.	peers	12.	beliefs
4.	subterranean	13.	labels
5.	Social control	14.	Deviance
6.	Edwin H. Sutherland	15.	dramatization
7.	reinforcement	16.	primary
8.	operant	17.	status
9.	drift	18.	appraisal

TRUE/FALSE

1.	T	16.	T
2.	F	17.	F
3.	T	18.	F
4.	T	19.	T
5.	T	20.	T
6.	F	21.	F
7.	F	22.	T
8.	F	23.	T
9.	T	24.	F
10.	F	25.	F
11.	T	26.	F
12.	T	27.	T
13.	T	28.	F
14.	F	29.	T
15.	T	30.	T

MULTIPLE CHOICE

1.	d	10.	c
2.	e	11.	b
3.	d	12.	a
4.	e	13.	d
5.	c	14.	b
6.	a	15.	c
7.	d	16.	b
8.	d	17.	e
9.	b	18.	c

MATCHING

1.	F
2.	I
3.	L
4.	C
5.	A
6.	D
7.	H
8.	B
9.	E
10.	G
11.	K
12.	J

78

9 Conflict Theory

LEARNING OBJECTIVES

1.   Compare the contributions of Willem Bonger, Ralf Dahrendorf and George Vold to developing a conflict theory of crime.

2.   Describe the origins and common objectives of conflict criminology.

3.   Describe the theory of the social reality of crime developed by Richard Quinney.

4.   Compare the research approach of conflict theory to consensus models.

5.   Identify the criticisms that have been directed toward conflict theory.

6.   Trace the development of Marxist (radical) criminology. Identify the views of Marxist criminologists.

7.   Compare the views and goals of instrumentalists to Structural Marxists.

8.   Explain the attempts to find links between radical criminology and concepts derived from traditional theories.

9.   Differentiate between a radical feminist perspective and a Marxist one.

10. Describe power-control theory's view towards crime and delinquency rates.

11. Identify and describe Marxist research which tends to be historical and analytical.

12. Explain the nature of the criticism which has been directed toward Marxist criminology.

13. Define left realism.

KEY TERMS AND CONCEPTS

Conflict theory
Production
Surplus value
Bourgeoisie
Proletariat
Power relations
Social reality of crime
Norm resistance
Dangerous classes
Patriarchy

Radical criminology
Marxist criminology
Economic structure
Instrumental Marxism
Contradictions
Privilege
Structural Marxism
Left realism
Preemptive deterrence
Marginalized

Marxist feminism
Gender conflict
Radical feminism
Paternalism
Power-control theory
Deconstructionism
Semiotics
Peace making criminology
Demystify
Restorative justice

NAMES TO KNOW

Karl Marx
Friedrich Engels
Georg Hegel
Willem Bonger
Ralf Dahrendorf
George Vold
David Greenberg
William Chambliss
Robert Seidman
Richard Quinney
David McDowall
David Jacobs
David Britt
Alan Lizotte
Thomas Arvanites
Michael Leiber
Katherine Jamieson
Richard Greenleaf
Lonn Lanza-Kaduce
Austin Turk
Theodore Chiricos
Gordon Waldo

Stephen Klein
Joan Petersilia
Susan Turner
Ian Taylor
Paul Walton
Jock Young
Anthony Platt
Paul Takagi
Hermand Schwendinger
Julia Schwendinger
Steven Spitzer
Barry Krisberg
David Friedrichs
Dennis Sullivan
Larry Tifft
Robert Bohm
Michael Lynch
W. Byron Groves
Gregg Barak
Timothy Carter
Donald Clelland

Drew Humphries
Rosalind Petchesky
A. T. Scull
Dennis Hoffman
Sidney Harring
Jackson Toby
Carl Klockars
John Lea
Martin Schwartz
Walter DeKeseredy
James Messerschmidt
Jane Siegel
Linda Meyer Williams
Ruth Alexander
Mary Odem
Steven Schlossman
Meda Chesney-Lind
John Hagan
Kevin Thompson
Harold Pepinsky
Peter Cordella

FILL-IN REVIEW

1. _____ theory assumes that crime is caused by the inter-group rivalry which exists in every society.

2. The writings of _____ and Engels had a great influence on the development of conflict thinking.

3. _____ is famous for his Marxist socialist concepts of crime causation which were first published in 1916.

4. _____ believed that modern society is organized into what he called <u>imperatively coordinated associations</u>.

5. As _____ says, "the whole political process of law making, law breaking and law enforcement becomes a direct reflection of deep-seated and fundamental conflicts between interest groups and their more general struggles for the control of the police power of the state."

6. Another motive of conflict theory is to describe the criminogenic influence of social and economic _____ --the ability of persons and groups to determine and control the behavior of others.

7. Richard Quinney integrated his beliefs about power, society, and criminality into a theory he referred to as the _____ _____ of crime.

8. Marxist criminologists view crime as a function of the _____ mode of production.

9. One group of Marxists is referred to as _____, who argue that capitalist justice serves the powerful and rich and enables them to impose their morality and standards of behavior on the entire society.

10. Barry Krisberg defines _____ as the possession of that which is valued by a particular social group in a given historical period.

11. Anthony Platt argues that given the ways in which this system has been used to repress and maintain the powerlessness of poor people, people of color, and young people, it is not too far-fetched to characterize many _____ as domestic war criminals.

12. _____ Marxists disagree with the view that the relationship between law and capitalism is unidimensional, always working for the rich and against the poor.

13. _____ involves co-opting deviants by making them part of the system--for example, a gang leader may be recruited to work with younger delinquents.

14. _____ involves segregating deviants into isolated geographic areas so that they can be easily controlled--for example, by creating a ghetto.

15. The Schwendingers believe that a _____ victim frequently experiences guilt because she has been raised in a sexist society and has internalized discriminatory norms.

16. _____ policing, like early fee-for-service constable systems or current civil court procedures, is a class based institution. It enables the rich to buy additional protection while the lower classes, who need protection the most, remain without adequate police services.

17. _____ Feminists view gender inequality as stemming from the unequal power of men and women in a capitalist society.

18. _____ feminists view the cause of female crime as originating with the onset of male supremacy, the subsequent subordination of women, male aggression, and the efforts of men to control females sexually.

19. According to John Hagan, within the _____ home, mothers are expected to control the behavior of their daughters while granting greater freedom to sons.

20. In _____ families--those which husband and wife share similar positions of power at home and in the work place--daughters gain a kind of freedom that reflects reduced parental control.

21. Marxists believe that the research conducted by mainstream liberal/positivist criminologists is designed to unmask the weak and powerless members of society so they can be better dealt with by the legal system--a process called _____.

22. _____ believe that language is value-laden and contains the same sort of inequities that are present in the rest of the social structure.

TRUE/FALSE

1. Marx wrote much on the topic of crime.

2. Bonger believed that if socialism can be achieved, then remaining crimes will be of the irrational psychopathic type caused by individual mental problems.

3. Dahrendorf embraces a Marxist conflict orientation.

4. Labeling theorists accepted the notion that crime is morally wrong.

5. Criminologists David Jacobs and David Britt found that state jurisdictions with significant levels of economic disparity were also the most likely to have the largest number of police shooting fatalities.

6. The development of radical theory can be traced to the National Deviancy Conference (NDC), formed in 1968 by a group of British sociologists.

7. Instrumentalists argue that the poor commit less crimes than the rich.

8. According to Herman Schwendinger and Julia Siegel Schwendinger, the basic laws of the land (such as constitutional laws) are based on the conditions that reproduce the class system as a whole.

9. Barry Krisberg has linked crime to the differentials in privilege that exist in capitalist society.

10. In general, Marxist research efforts have failed to yield evidence linking operations of the justice system to class bias.

11. Structural Marxists argue that law is the exclusive domain of the rich.

12. To a structuralist, anti-trust legislation is designed the support select capitalists in their domination of the system.

13. One highly regarded structural Marxist work is Spitzer's Marxian theory of deviance.

14. Spitzer finds that law in the capitalist system defines as criminal any person who disturbs the capitalist modes of appropriating the product of human labor.

15. Spitzer argues that one mechanism that capitalist societies create to deal with those who oppose its operation is to contain deviants by making them sensitive to the needs of the system--for example, through legalization of abortion procedures.

16. The Schwendingers' research approach illustrates the Marxian stress on quantitative statistical evidence and their disdain for analysis and interpretation of social process.

17. Michael Rustigan analyzed historical records to show that law reform in nineteenth-century England was largely a response to pressure from the church to make the punishment for moral offenses more severe.

18. Sidney Harring has provided one of the more important analyses of the development of modern policing, showing how police developed as an antilabor force that provided muscle for industrialists at the turn of the century.

82

19.   The Pinkertons were hired by labor unions to supply intelligence in the "just war against capitalists."

20.   Jackson Toby argues that the crimes of the rich are more reprehensible and less understandable than those who in live in poverty. Criminality and immoral behavior occur at every social level, but Toby believes the relatively advantaged contribute disproportionately to hidden crime and delinquency.

21.   Carl Klockars scoffs at critical thinkers who charge that efforts by the government to create social reforms are disguised attempts to control the underclass. Is it logical to believe that giving people more rights is a trick to allow greater control to be exerted over them?

22.   Marxist scholars charge that critics rely on "traditional" variables such as "class" and "poverty" in their analysis of radical thought. While important, these do not reflect the key issues in the structural and economic process. In fact, like crime, they too may be outcome of the capitalist system.

23.   According to sociologists Martin Schwartz and Walter DeKeserdy, the core premise of left realism is that radical criminologists have ignored the victimization of the working class in order to focus on upper class crime.

24.   Marxist Feminists view gender inequality as a function of the socialization of females by male employers, as well as political and religious leaders.

25.   Meda Chesney-Lind found that police in Chicago were likely to arrest male adolescents for sexual activity and to ignore the same behavior among female delinquents.

26.   Hagan and his associates found that when both father and mother hold equally valued managerial positions, the difference between the rates of their daughter's and son's delinquency is greatest.

27.   Power control theory implies that middle class youth of both sexes will have higher crime rates than their lower class peers.

MULTIPLE CHOICE

1.   Which of the following is considered a "true crime" according to conflict theorists:
        a.   burglary
        b.   robbery
        c.   assault
        d.   substandard housing

2.   Which of the following is true concerning the interests of conflict theorists:
        a.   they examine bias and discrimination in the operations of the justice system
        b.   they compare the crime rates of powerless groups with those of the elite classes
        c.   they attempt to chart the historical development of criminal law and to identify laws created with the intent of preserving the power of the elite at the expense of the poor
        d.   both "a" and "b"
        e.   all of the above ("a" thru "c")

3. Bonger believed that:
   a. not all people desire wealth
   b. no act is naturally immoral or criminal
   c. society was divided into three groups: the haves, the marginals, and the have-nots
   d. attempts to control law violations through force are a sign of a strong society
   e. it is the absolute amount of wealth that affects crime

4. Dahrendorf argued that:
   a. Marx foresaw the changes that have occurred in the laboring classes
   b. the working class of today... is a stratum differentiated by numerous subtle and not so subtle distinctions
   c. Marx's concept of a cohesive proletarian class has proved accurate
   d. both "a" and "c"
   e. all of the above ("a" thru "c")

5. Dahrendorf believed that:
   a. every society is at every point subject to processes of change; social change is everywhere
   b. every society displays at every point dissent and conflict; social conflict is everywhere
   c. every element in a society renders a contribution to its disintegration and change
   d. all of the above ("a" thru "c")
   e. none of the above ("a" thru "c")

6. Vold's model:
   a. can be used to explain all types of crime
   b. is limited to situations in which rival group loyalties collide
   c. explains impulsive, irrational acts
   d. all of the above ("a" thru "c")
   e. none of the above ("a" thru "c")

7. The theory developed by Richard Quinney involved:
   a. application of criminal definitions
   b. development of behavior patterns in relation to criminal definition
   c. construction of criminal conceptions
   d. all of the above ("a" thru "c")
   e. none of the above ("a" thru "c")

8. Richard Quinney maintained that:
   a. law is an abstract body of rules that represents an absolute moral code
   b. criminals are people who have come up short in the struggle for success
   c. law violations can be viewed as religious acts
   d. all of the above ("a" thru "c")
   e. none of the above ("a" thru "c")

9. The aim of conflict theory is to describe how:
   a. law represents the values of the majority of landowners and merchants
   b. legal codes are designed to create a just society through attracting the right "people"
   c. by breaking the law, criminals are predators who violate the rights of others
   d. class differentials produce an ecology of human behavior that favors the wealthy and powerful over the poor and weak

10. Refutation of conflict theory includes evidence that:
   a. it is too realistic
   b. data indicates a strong relationship exists between unemployment and crime rates
   c. the justice system is not class or race biased
   d. all of the above ("a" thru "c")
   e. none of the above ("a" thru "c")

11. One analysis of crime in the African country of Tanzania found that when the free enterprise system was replaced by a socialist society, the crime rate:
   a. actually increased
   b. remained the same
   c. for property crimes actually decreased
   d. for violent crimes actually decreased

12. During the late 1960s and early 1970s, which of the following were factors which supported criticism of the "ruling class":
   a. war in Vietnam
   b. prison struggles
   c. civil rights movement
   d. all of the above ("a" thru "c")
   e. none of the above ("a" thru "c")

13. As a general rule Marxist criminologists:
   a. are strongly committed to formal theory construction
   b. are in favor of empirical testing
   c. are in search of an objective social science
   d. urge the adoption of an ideological basis for criminological scholarship

14. Privilege, according to Barry Krisberg includes:
   a. rights such as life, liberty, and happiness
   b. traits such as intelligence, sensitivity, and humanity
   c. material goods such as monetary wealth, luxuries, and land
   d. all of the above ("a" thru "c")
   e. none of the above ("a" thru "c")

15. To a(n) _____, the law is designed to keep the capitalist system operating in an efficient manner and anyone, who "rocks the boat" is targeted for sanction.
   a. ritualist
   b. instrumentalist
   c. structuralist
   d. ideologue

16. Stephen Spitzer finds that law in the capitalist system defines as deviant any person who calls into question:
   a. the process of socialization for productive and nonproductive roles
   b. the social conditions under which capitalist production takes place
   c. patterns of distribution and consumption in capitalist society
   d. all of the above ("a" thru "c")
   e. none of the above ("a" thru "c")

17. Spitzer maintains that one mechanism that capitalist societies use to deal with those who oppose its operation is to _____ formerly deviant or illegal acts by absorbing them into the mainstream of society.
    a. normalize
    b. convert
    c. contain
    d. discredit

18. Marxist research is:
    a. statistical
    b. rigorously prescriptive
    c. methodological
    d. situational

19. The impetus behind Pinkerton's private police force was:
    a. to respond to the growth of population in urban areas
    b. to foster ethnocentric delinquency
    c. to supplement the services provided by Chicago's police force
    d. to advanced organize crime among the wealthy
    e. to structure the push toward normality for the "dangerous classes"

20. Meda Chesney-Lind found that:
    a. the court ordered physical examinations in about 60 percent of the male cases and only in about 30 percent of the females cases
    b. females were more likely to be sent to a detention facility before trial than males
    c. a lower percentage of females than males were institutionalized for similar delinquent acts
    d. all of the above ("a" thru "c")
    e. none of the above ("a" thru "c")

21. Which of the following is true about Marxist criminologists:
    a. they frequently use classical social science tools
    b. they believe that positivist research is designed to unmask the powerless
    c. their research tends to be quantitative and empirical rather than historical and analytical
    d. all of the above are true ("a" thru "c")
    e. none of the above are true ("a" thru "c")

22. A view of Carl Klockars toward Marxist criminology:
    a. it is trustworthy as a social movement
    b. it is unpredictable
    c. it ignores objective reality
    d. it explains criminality in states that have abolished the private ownership of the means of production

MATCHING

_____	1.	Stephen Spitzer	A.	"Ultimate capitalists"
_____	2.	Peacemaking criminology	B.	Female "sex delinquent"
_____	3.	George Vold	C.	"Double marginality"
_____	4.	Labeling theory	D.	Crime is a function of privilege
_____	5.	Street criminals	E.	Structural Marxist
_____	6.	Richard Quinney	F.	The social reality of crime
_____	7.	Eugenics	G.	Proletariat
_____	8.	National Deviancy Conference	H.	Quakerism to Zen
_____	9.	Marxist Feminists	I.	Development of radical theory
_____	10.	Instrumental Marxists	J.	Adapted conflict theory to criminology
_____	11.	Workers	K.	Want to demystify law and justice"
_____	12.	Barry Krisberg	L.	"Nuts, sluts, and perverts"

ESSAY QUESTIONS

1. What are the concerns of conflict theorists?

2. Identify the contributions of Willem Bonger..

3. Describe Dahrendorf's model of conflict.

4. What kind of crimes can be explained by Vold's model?

5. Describe the factors associated with the emergence of conflict theory in the sixties and early seventies.

6. Identify Quinney's six propositions in his theory of social reality. What are the factors in the formulation of criminal definitions?

7. What are the research interests of conflict theorists?

8. Identify the criticisms directed toward the conflict view.

9. Describe the views of Marxist criminologists toward causes of crime.

10. Trace the development of radical criminology.

11. How do instrumentalists view the criminal law and criminal justice system? Summarize Quinney's Marxist theory. Characterize the Schwendingers' view of law.

12. How do structural Marxists differ from instrumentalists?

13. According to Spitzer, how do capitalist societies deal with those who oppose its operation?

14. Compare radical feminist theory of the causes of female crime to Marxists Feminists.

15. What is the meaning and importance of the findings of Meda Chesney-Lind?

16.   From a power-control approach, compare and contrast paternalistic homes to egalitarian families.

17.   Characterize Marxist research. Identify the common themes underpinning their research.

18.   What are the major criticisms of Marxist criminologists?

19.   What is the approach of left realism?

88

CHAPTER NINE ANSWER SECTION

FILL-IN REVIEW

1.	Conflict	12.	Structural
2.	Marx	13.	Conversion
3.	Bonger	14.	Containment
4.	Dahrendorf	15.	rape
5.	Vold	16.	Private
6.	power	17.	Marxist
7.	social reality	18.	Radical
8.	capitalist	19.	paternalistic
9.	instrumentalists	20.	egalitarian
10.	privilege	21.	correctionalism
11.	criminologists	22.	Deconstructionists

TRUE/FALSE

1.	F	15.	F
2.	T	16.	F
3.	F	17.	F
4.	F	18.	T
5.	T	19.	F
6.	T	20.	F
7.	F	21.	T
8.	T	22.	T
9.	T	23.	T
10.	F	24.	F
11.	F	25.	F
12.	F	26.	F
13.	T	27.	T
14.	T		

MULTIPLE CHOICE

1.	d	12.	d
2.	e	13.	d
3.	b	14.	d
4.	b	15.	c
5.	d	16.	d
6.	b	17.	a
7.	d	18.	d
8.	b	19.	c
9.	d	20.	b
10.	c	21.	e
11.	a	22.	c

MATCHING

1.	E
2.	H
3.	J
4.	L
5.	A
6.	F
7.	B
8.	I
9.	C
10.	K
11.	G
12.	D

10 Integrated Theories

LEARNING OBJECTIVES

1. Explain reasons for the recent popularity of integrated theory.

2. Compare and contrast multi-factor, latent trait and life course theories.

3. Describe the theory of social development crafted by Joseph Weis and his associates.

4. Describe Elliott's Integrated Theory and how it has been tested.

5. Identify the insights of integrated structural Marxist theory.

6. Define the assumptions underpinning the Wilson-Herrnstein model.

7. Explain Gottfredson and Hirschi's General Theory of Crime. Evaluate its value.

8. Describe how the Glueck's research is being used today.

9. Explain important concepts associated with the life course perspective.

10. Describe the elements of life-course theories developed by Farrington, Thornberry and Laub and Sampson.

KEY TERMS AND CONCEPTS

Multi-factor theories
Latent trait theories
Life course theories
Differential anticipation theory
Social development model
Prosocial bonds
Integrated structural theory
General theory of crime
Impulsive personality
Self control

Life cycle
Early onset
Continuity of crime
Propensity
Opportunity
Social interactional theory
Problem behavior syndrome
Pathways
Authority conflicted pathway
Covert pathway

Overt pathway
Adolescent-limited
Life-course persistent
Pseudomaturity
Interactional theory
Cognitive perspective
Turning points
Age-graded theory
Social capital

90

NAMES TO KNOW

David Rowe
D. Wayne Osgood
W. Alan Nicewander
Daniel Glazer
Joseph Weis
Richard Catalano
J. David Hawkins
Delbert Elliott
David Huizinga
Suzanne Ageton
Mark Colvin
John Pauly
Lee Ellis
James Q. Wilson
Richard Herrnstein
Travis Hirschi
Michael Gottfredson

John Gibbs
Dennis Giever
Marc LeBlanc
Scott Menard
Sharon Wofford
Graham Ousey
David Aday, Jr.
Julie Horney
Gerald Patterson
Sheldon Glueck
Eleanor Glueck
John Laub
Robert Sampson
Rolf Loeber
Helene Raskin White
Erich Labouvie
Terrie Moffitt

Paul Mazzerole
Charles Dean
Deborah Baskin
Ira Sommers
Henry Brownstein
Barry Spunt
Susan Crimmins
Sandra Langley
Stephen Hansell
David Farrington
Terence Thornberry
Daniel Nagin
Raymond Paternoster
Eloise Dunlop
Bruce Johnson

FILL-IN REVIEW

1   Why do some criminals reduce criminal activity and then resume it once again? This approach is sometimes referred to as _____ criminology.

2.   The multi-factor approach helps criminologists explain both criminal career formation and _____ from crime.

3.   While the propensity to commit crime is stable, the _____ to commit crime fluctuates over time.

4.   In contrast to the latent trait view, _____ course theories hold that the propensity to commit crimes changes over time; it is a developmental process.

5.   According to the Elliott view, perceptions of _____ (the condition which occurs when a person begins to believe they cannot achieve success through conventional means, such as education or job), inadequate socialization, and living in a socially disorganized area leads youths to develop weak bonds with conventional groups, activities and norms.

6.   Biosocial theorist Lee Ellis maintains that the physical-chemical functioning of the _____ is responsible for all human behavior and _____ function is controlled by genetic and environmental factors of crime.

7.   According to _____ and Herrnstein, all human behavior, including criminality, is determined by its perceived consequences.

8.   In an important work, A General Theory of Crime, _____ writing with Gottfredson, has modified and redefined some of the principals articulated in his social control theory by integrating the concepts of control with those of biosocial, psychological, routine activities and rational choice theories.

9. The explanations for individual differences in the tendency to commit criminal acts can be found in a person's level of self-control. People with limited self-control tend to be _____, insensitive, physical, risk-taking, short-sighted, and non-verbal.

10. A number of themes are now emerging. One is that the seeds of a criminal career are planted early in life: early _____ of deviance is a strong predictor of later criminality.

11. There has been a great deal of research on the relationship of age and crime and the activities of chronic offenders. This body of scholarship has prompted interested in the life _____ of crime: what causes the commencement of criminality? What sustains a criminal career over the course of a person's life?

12. While at Harvard University in the 1930's, Sheldon and Eleanor _____ had popularized research on the life cycle of delinquent careers.

13. In their studies on delinquency prevention, Gerald Patterson and his colleagues at the Oregon Social Learning Center found that poor parental _____ and monitoring was a key to the commencement of criminality in early childhood.

14. Criminality may best be understood from the life course view as one of many social problems faced by "at risk" youths. Criminality may be part of a problem behavior _____ (PBS).

15. White found that delinquents and drug abusers actually could fall into one of several behaviorally defined groups: some were involved in delinquency but not drug abuse; others used drugs but were crime free; some were _____ who engaged in both delinquency and drug abuse.

16. Using data taken from a longitudinal cohort study conducted in Pittsburgh Rolf Loeber and his associates are now formulating the _____ to crime traveled by at-risk youth.

17. While considerable research interest is now being devoted to female offenders, there has actually been very little research charting the life course of one subset of this group: _____ female street criminals.

18. Early data seems to support what is already known about delinquent-criminal career patterns: that early commencement predicts later offending; that there is _____ in crime (juvenile offenders are the ones most likely to become adult criminals) and that chronic offenders commit a significant portion of all crimes.

19. The results of the _____ study have been quite important because they show that many of the same patterns found in the U.S. are repeated in a cross-national sample: the existence of chronic offenders; constancy of offending; early commencement leading to persistent criminality.

20. Farrington argues that the chance of offending in any particular situation depends on the perception of the _____ and benefits of crime and non-crime alternatives.

21. Interactional theory is considered "age graded" because it incorporates an element of the _____ in psychology: as people mature they pass through different stages of reasoning and sophistication.

22.	In an important new work, <u>Crime in the Making</u>, Robert Sampson and John Laub, identify the "turning _____" in a criminal career. They find that the stability of delinquent behavior can be effected by events which occur later in life, even after a chronic delinquent career has been undertaken.

24.	According to Sampson and Laub, these life events help people build social _____- positive relations with individuals and institutions which are life sustaining.

TRUE/FALSE

1.	While early criminologists have tended to be more specialized, modern criminologists have readily embraced the theoretical work of their colleagues.

2.	The development of large computerized data bases and software which facilitates statistical analysis now makes theory integration practical.

3.	Multi-factor theories tend to divide the world simply into "criminals" and "noncriminals," those who have a crime producing condition and those who don't.

4.	Integrated theories have also helped focus on the occasional or sporadic offender (for example, the Philadelphia cohort).

5.	Single factor theories have trouble explaining why only a relatively few of the many individuals exposed to criminogenic influences in the environment actually become chronic offenders.

6.	The negative association between past and future criminality detected in the cohort studies of career criminals may reflect the presence of several underlying criminogenic traits.

7.	Life course theories recognize that even as people mature the critical factors which influence their behavior remain the same.

8.	Life-course and multi-factor theories tend to stress the influence of inter-personal and structural factors.

9.	Efforts to create multi-factor theories are new.

10.	Weis's model can account for both the high crime rates found in lower-class areas as well as the influence of critical agents of the social order on criminal behavior.

11.	Elliott and his colleagues tested their theoretical model with data taken from a national youth survey of approximately 1800 youth who were interviewed annually over a three year period.

12.	The picture Elliott draws of the teenage delinquent is quite different from the depiction Weis portrays in his Social Development model.

13.	All multi-factor views of crime rely solely on mainstream concepts.

14.	According to integrated structural theory, it is naive to believe that a crime control policy can be formulated without regard for its basic root causes.

15. Wilson and Herrnstein ignore the influence of social factors on criminality.

16. Wilson and Herrnstein view harsh punishment as the answer to the crime problem.

17. In their general theory Gottfredson and Hirschi consider the criminal offender and the criminal act as separate concepts.

18. Gottfredson and Hirschi trace the root cause of poor self-control to genetic influences.

19. Gottfredson and Hirschi claim that the principles of self-control theory can be used to explain all varieties of criminal behavior and all the social and behavioral correlates of crime.

20. Gottfredson and Hirschi maintain that the relatively few white-collar criminals lack self-control in the manner rapists and burglars lack self-control.

21. According to life course theories, the best predictor of future criminality is past criminality.

22. The Glueck's research was closely examined for over thirty years.

23. Most criminological theories portray crime as the cause of social problems rather than their result.

24. According to Farrington's theoretical model, being nervous, withdrawn and having few friends is positively related to adolescent and teenage offending but negatively related to adult social dysfunction.

MULTIPLE CHOICE

1. It has become important to chart the natural history of a criminal career. Why do some offenders escalate their criminal activities while others decrease or limit law violations? This approach is sometimes referred to as _____ criminology.
   a. maturation
   b. process
   c. transaction
   d. growth
   e. developmental

2. Which of the following variables are used in multi-factor theories:
   a. structural
   b. socialization
   c. conflict
   d. individual
   e. all of the above ("a" thru "d") are used in multi-factor theories.

3. Life course theories recognize that as people mature the factors which influence their behavior also undergo change. In adulthood, _____ relations may be the most critical influence.
   a. employment
   b. marital
   c. peer
   d. family

94

4. Differential anticipation theory was designed by:
    a.   D. Wayne Osgood
    b.   David Rowe
    c.   W. Alan Nicewander
    d.   Daniel Glazer
    e.   none of the above ("a" thru "c")

5. Weis's model uses elements of both _____ and social structure theories.
    a.   conflict
    b.   control
    c.   consensus
    d.   strain
    e.   environmental

6. The view of Elliott, Huizinga and Ageton combines the features of _____, social learning, and control theories into a single theoretical model.
    a.   conflict
    b.   control
    c.   consensus
    d.   strain
    e.   environmental

7. Biosocial theorist Lee Ellis maintains that:
    a.   genetic predisposition should be the focus of major research efforts
    b.   neurological defects in the left cortex are responsible for violent criminal behavior
    c.   social influences on spinal function encompass both physical and experiential factors
    d.   the physical-chemical functioning of the brain is responsible for all human behavior

8. One of the most widely read and analyzed works in the criminological literature is James Q. Wilson and Richard Herrnstein's book:
    a.   A General Theory of Crime
    b.   Crime and Human Nature
    c.   Behavioral Approaches to Crime and Delinquency
    d.   Deviant Behavior

9. One of the more controversial assertions in Wilson-Herrnstein's model is that the relationship between crime and _____ is "robust and significant."
    a.   age
    b.   sex
    c.   class
    d.   intelligence
    e.   culture

10. Wilson and Herrnstein answer(s) to the crime problem:
    a.   making punishment more severe
    b.   restructuring the justice system
    c.   strengthening the family
    d.   all of the above ("a" thru "c")
    e.   none of the above ("a" thru "c")

11. In their general theory Gottfredson and Hirschi consider:
    a. the criminal offender and the criminal act as separate concepts
    b. the justice system as an important source of criminality
    c. the ideological basis of crime control
    d. the relationship between capitalism and family structure

12. To Gottfredson and Hirschi, people with limited self-control tend to be:
    a. sensitive
    b. mental
    c. verbal
    d. impulsive
    e. none of the above ("a" thru "d")

13. According to Gottfredson and Hirschi, one of the six elements of self control is:
    a. strong commitment to class values
    b. positive attitude toward life
    c. inclination for empirical testing
    d. tendency to be diligent, tenacious and persistent
    e. possession of an objective mind

14. One of the questions with the "general theory" developed by Gottfredson and Hirschi is:
    a. too focused on social ecological patterns in the crime rate
    b. acknowledges the moral concept of "right and wrong" which is a cornerstone of recent writings on the social bond
    c. traits such as sagacity, sensitivity, and humanity are ignored
    d. implies that offenders suffer from a personality defect that makes them impulsive and rash
    e. assumes that people change

15. Gerald Patterson and his colleagues at the Oregon Social Learning Center found that antisocial behavior was sustained in middle childhood by:
    a. commitment to a deviant peer group
    b. ineffective parental disciple and monitoring
    c. rejection by conventional peers and academic failure
    d. all of the above ("a" thru "c")
    e. none of the above ("a" thru "c")

16. Labouvie and White found that among delinquents and drug abusers:
    a. some were involved in delinquency but not drug abuse
    b. some used drugs but were crime free
    c. some were "generalists" who engaged in both delinquency and drug abuse
    d. all of the above ("a" thru "c")
    e. none of the above ("a" thru "c")

17. The _____ pathway consists of an escalation of aggressive acts beginning with aggression leading to physical fighting to violence.
    a. overt
    b. manifest
    c. authority
    d. conflict
    e. covert

96

18.   Baskin and Sommers found that about _____ percent of violent female offenders begin their criminal career at a very early age.
        a.   5
        b.   20
        c.   45
        d.   60
        e.   none of the above ("a" thru "d")

19.   Farrington found that by age _____ the chronic offender is already exhibiting anti-social behavior including dishonesty and aggressiveness.
        a.   3
        b.   5
        c.   8
        d.   13
        e.   19

20.   Farrington found that (a) factor(s) which "protected" high risk youth from even beginning a criminal career included:
        a.   having many friends
        b.   a personality which rendered them somewhat shy
        c.   being highly regarded by their father
        d.   all of the above ("a" thru "c")
        e.   none of the above ("a" thru "c")

21.   Farrington found that (a) factor(s) which helped offenders to desist included:
        a.   employment
        b.   marriage
        c.   relocation
        d.   all of the above are true ("a" thru "c")
        e.   none of the above are true ("a" thru "c")

22.   Thornberry agrees with _____ that the onset of crime can be traced to a deterioration of the social bond during adolescence, marked by a weakened attachment to parents, commitment to school and belief in conventional values.
        a.   Carl Klockars
        b.   John Laub
        c.   Delbert Elliott
        d.   Travis Hirschi
        e.   none of the above ("a" thru "d")

MATCHING

____	1.	marriage and career	A.	Baskin and Sommers
____	2.	Cambridge study	B.	Life sustaining positive relations
____	3.	material production	C.	group of clustering anti-social behaviors
____	4.	Glueck's research	D.	Hirschi and Gottfredson
____	5.	Violent female street criminals	E.	"turning points"
____	6.	powerful physique	F.	mesomorphs
____	7.	social capital	G.	Thornberry's model
____	8.	Covert pathway	H.	Farrington
____	9.	problem behavior syndrome	I.	lying, shoplifting, setting fires, pickpocketing
____	10.	Discontinuity	J.	integrated structural theory
____	11.	Rochester Youth Survey	K.	desistance
____	12.	Self-control	L.	precursor of the life course school

ESSAY QUESTIONS

1. How are integrated theories useful for understanding criminality?

2. Which theories use structural level variables?

3. Compare life course theories to latent trait approach.

4. Describe the assumptions, methodology and findings of the research of Elliott and his colleagues.

5. What is the solution to the crime problem according to Wilson and Herrnstein?

6. What makes people crime prone according to Gottfredson and Hirschi?

7. Name the six elements of self control.

9. What are the problems with the "general theory" developed by Gottfredson and Hirschi?

10. How important was the work by Sheldon and Eleanor Glueck?

11. Describe research efforts which show that criminogenic influences undergo change and development

12. How does Farrington describe the characteristics of the chronic offender?

13. Identify the factors that Farrington found which predict the discontinuity of criminal offenses.

14. Identify and explain five out of the seven major characteristics of Farrington's theoretical model.

15. Why is Thornberry's model considered an "age graded" approach?

CHAPTER TEN ANSWER SECTION

FILL-IN REVIEW

1.	developmental		13.	discipline
2.	desistence		14.	syndrome
3.	opportunity		15.	"generalists"
4.	life		16.	pathways
5.	strain		17.	violent
6.	brain, brain		18.	continuity
7.	Wilson		19.	Cambridge
8.	Hirschi		20.	costs
9.	impulsive		21.	cognitive
10.	onset		22.	points
11.	cycle		23.	capital
12.	Glueck			

TRUE/FALSE

1.	F	14.	T
2.	T	15.	F
3.	F	16.	F
4.	F	17.	T
5.	T	18.	F
6.	F	19.	T
7.	F	20.	T
8.	T	21.	T
9.	F	22.	F
10.	T	23.	F
11.	T	24.	F
12.	F		
13.	F		

MULTIPLE CHOICE

1.	e	12.	d
2.	e	13.	d
3.	b	14.	d
4.	d	15.	c
5.	b	16.	d
6.	d	17.	a
7.	d	18.	d
8.	b	19.	c
9.	d	20.	b
10.	c	21.	d
11.	a	22.	c

MATCHING

1.	E
2.	H
3.	J
4.	L
5.	A
6.	F
7.	B
8.	I
9.	C
10.	K
11.	G
12.	D

11 Violent Crime

LEARNING OBJECTIVES

1. Define the concept of subculture of violence and evaluate its ability to explain violent crime.

2. Evaluate the importance of geography in explaining violence.

3. Evaluate the link between violence and both substance abuse and firearm availability.

4. Describe the history, incidence, and causes of rape.

5. Explore the problems between law and the crime of rape.

6. Describe the nature and extent of murder.

7. Explain the various relationships between killers and victims.

8. Explain the possible causes of child and spouse abuse.

9. Identify and describe robber typologies.

10. Define and describe hate crime.

11. Identify the precipitants to workplace violence

KEY TERMS AND CONCEPTS

Brutalization process
Violent performances
Virulency
Eros
thanatos
Subculture of violence
Disputatiousness
Ganging
Regional values
Psychopharmacological
Economic compulsive
behavior
Systemic link
Instrumental violence
Expressive violence
Heiress stealing
Anger rape
Power rape
Sadistic rape
Date rape

Marital rape
Consent
Shield laws
Corroboration
Feticide
Premeditation
Felony murder
Homicide networks
Thrill killing
Gang killing
Cult killing
Serial murder
Mass murder
Assault
Battery
Child abuse
Sexual abuse
Spouse abuse
Professional robber
Opportunist robber

Addict robber
Alcoholic robber
Hate or bias crime
Thrill-seeking hate crime
Reactive hate crime
Mission hate crime
Workplace violence
Political violence
Terrorism
Convictional criminals
Guerrilla
Revolutionary terrorism
Political terrorism
Nationalistic terrorism
Nonpolitical terrorism
State-sponsored terrorism
Death squads
Structural violence
Genocide

NAMES TO KNOW

David Courtwright
Laura Bender
Dorothy Otnow lewis
Gerald patterson
Murray Straus
Lonnie Athens
Sigmund Freud
Konrad Lorenz
Marvin Wolfgang
Franco Ferracuti
Scott Decker
Carolyn Block
Raymond Gastil
Colin Loftin
Robert Hill
Paul Goldstein

Susan Brownmiller
A. Nicholas Groth
Raymond Knight
Diana Russell
Richard Felson
Marvin Krohn
Angela Browne
Kirk Williams
Margaret Zahn
Philip Sagi
David Luckenbill
Richard Block
Charles Ewing
Jack Levin
James Alan Fox

Belea Keeney
Kathleen Heide
Philip Jenkins
Richard Gelles
Jeanne Hernandez
Martin Schwartz
Walter DeKeseredy
John Conklin
Jack McDevitt
John King
Stephen Schafer
Danile Georges-Abeyie
Ronald Kramer
Ervin Staub
Austin Turk

FILL-IN REVIEW

1.   Some experts suggest that there are violence prone _____ within society whose members value force, routinely carry weapons, and consider violence to have an acceptable place in social interaction.

2.   Sigmund Freud believed that human aggression and violence were produced by _____ drives.

3.   _____- can be expressed externally (as violence and sadism) or internally (as suicide, alcoholism, or other self-destructive habits).

4.   Violence is considered "appropriate" behavior within culturally defined conflict situations in which an individual has been offended by a negative outcome in a dispute and seeks reparations through violent means (_____).

5.   Diana Russell describes the _____ mystique--the belief that males learn to separate their sexual feelings from needs for love, respect, and affection.

6.   In most jurisdictions, it is essential to prove that the rape attack was forced and that the victim did not give voluntary _____ to her attacker.

7.   Most (48) states and the federal government have developed _____ laws, which protect women from being questioned about their sexual history unless it is judged to have a direct bearing on the case.

8.   Traditionally, a legally married husband could not be charged with raping his own wife; this was referred to as the marital _____.

9.   There is no _____ of limitations in murder cases.

10. To prove that a murder has taken place, most state jurisdictions require prosecutors prove that the accused intentionally and with _____ desired the death of the victim.

11. _____ means that the killing was considered beforehand and suggests that it was motivated by more than a simple desire to engage in an act of violence.

12. _____ means that the killing was planned and decided on after careful thought rather than carried out on impulse.

13. _____ murders occur during rapes, robberies, and burglaries.

14. _____ killing involves impulsive violence motivated by the killer's decision to kill a stranger as an act of "daring" or recklessness.

15. Serial killers operate over a long period of time and can be distinguished from the _____ murderer who kills many victims in a single violent outburst.

16. The FBI defines serious assault, or _____ assault, as "an unlawful attack by one person upon another for the purpose of inflicting severe bodily injury."

17. _____ _____ describes any physical or emotional trauma to a child for which no reasonable explanation can be found.

18. The common-law definition of _____ is "the taking or attempting to take anything of value from the care, custody or control of a person or persons by force or threat of force or violence and/or by putting the victim in fear."

19. _____ crimes are violent acts directed toward a particular person or members of a group merely because the targets share a discernable racial, ethnic, religious, or gender characteristic.

20. According to one national commission _____ is a "tactic or technique by means of which a violent act or the threat thereof is used for the prime purpose of creating overwhelming fear for coercive purposes."

21. Upper class political terrorism has been manifested in the _____ squads operating in Latin America and Asia.

TRUE/FALSE

1. Because evidence exists that violent offenders are more prone to psychosis than other people, a superordinate clinical diagnosis has been developed which can characterize their misbehavior.

2. Freud believed that aggression could be successfully treated.

3. There are three ways in which drug abuse impacts on violence.

4. Today rape is considered to be a forceful expression of sexuality.

5.   Acquaintance rapes are typically more violent than stranger rapes.

6.   Rape was a common occurrence in early civilization.

7.   Sexual assault laws outlaw any type of forcible sex, including homosexual rape.

8.   There is no statute of limitations in murder cases.

9.   The principals in homicide usually know one another.

10.   Gang killings occur when members are ordered to kill peers who are suspected of deviating from the leader's teachings.

11.   Angela Brown and Kirk Williams looked at homicide trends over a 12 year period (1976-1987) and found that while the number of unmarried men killed by their partners increased, the rate of women killed by the men they lived with decreased slightly.

12.   Recent research seems to support Wolfgang's victim precipitation model.

13.   There is a distinct type of serial killer.

14.   Most experts view serial killers as sociopaths who from early childhood demonstrated bizarre behavior.

15.   Levin and Fox suggest that up to twenty serial killers are active in a given year accounting for up to 240 killings or about one percent of the total number of homicides.

16.   Catching serial killers is often a matter of luck.

17.   Abusive parents can be categorized by sex, age, and educational level.

18.   Severe wife beating fell into disfavor by the mid-nineteenth century.

19.   Spouse abuse among men who have seen military service is extremely high.

20.   Robbery is punished severely because of the value of the items taken.

21.   McDevitt found that a majority of hate crimes were minor incidents involving simple assaults or petty larcenies.

22.   Information on the extent of hate crimes is just becoming available.

23.   Schafer refers to those who violate the law because they believe their actions will ultimately benefit society as convictional criminals.

24.   According to Ronald Kramer, structural violence is another form of state-sponsored terrorism which involves the physical harm caused by the unequal distribution of wealth.

25.   It is often easy to separate violent political crimes from interpersonal crimes of violence.

MULTIPLE CHOICE

1. Recent research disputes the notion of a _____ culture of lethal violence and murder.
    a. northern
    b. southern
    c. western
    d. eastern

2. Usually <u>excluded</u> from the crime of rape:
    a. forced participation in fellatio
    b. coerced participation of a male in intercourse or other sexual activity by a female
    c. coerced sexual intercourse induced by the threat of economic harm
    d. all of the above ("a" thru "c")
    e. none of the above ("a" thru "c")

3. It has been estimated that _____ percent of all college women are victims of rape or attempted rape.
    a. 20
    b. 46
    c. 70
    d. 90
    e. 95

4. Which of the following is <u>true</u> about the incidence of rape:
    a. most reported rapes occur in the northwest
    b. the police clear by arrest approximately 25 percent of all reported rape offenses
    c. the lowest reported rates of rape occur during December, January, and February
    d. all of the above ("a" thru "c")

5. Konrad Lorenz developed a theory in his famous book, <u>On Aggression</u>, that argues that:
    a. aggressive energy is produced by familial instincts that are dependent on environmental forces for triggering
    b. aggression is rarely fatal among lower species
    c. in the animal kingdom, aggression usually serves a destructive purpose
    d. humans have an inhibition against fatal violence

6. Dr. A. Nicholas Groth found that the _____ rapist is bound up in ritual.
    a. anger
    b. power
    c. normative
    d. religious
    e. sadistic

7. _____ or actual malice is the state of mind assumed to exist when someone kills another person in the absence of any apparent provocation.
    a. Implied
    b. Constructive
    c. Transferred
    d. Express
    e. Direct

8. Murder in the _____ degree occurs when a person kills another after premeditation and deliberation.
    a. first
    b. second
    c. third
    d. none of the above ("a" thru "c")

9. Which of the following is true about murder:
    a. murder victims tend to be females
    b. murder victims tend to be under 18 years of age
    c. murder tends to be an intraracial crime
    d. all of the above ("a" thru "c")
    e. none of the above ("a" thru "c")

10. Which of the following is true about murder patterns:
    a. most victims knew their assailants
    b. most murders involved knives or cutting instruments
    c. about 60 percent occurred during the commission of a felony such as a burglary
    d. all of the above ("a" thru "c")
    e. none of the above ("a" thru "c")

11. Which of the following is true about murder rates:
    a. highest in large cities
    b. highest in the South
    c. highest during the summer months
    d. all of the above ("a" thru "c")
    e. none of the above ("a" thru "c")

12. One type of serial killer is the _____, or sadistic child killer, who gains sexual satisfaction from torturing and killing young children.
    a. pedofillic
    b. mysoped
    c. babihate
    d. childoerotica
    e. adolespent

13. According to Levin and Fox:
    a. about 350 mass murderers are active across the United States today
    b. mass murderers are actually ordinary citizens driven to extreme acts
    c. mass murderers are rarely motivated by profit or expediency
    d. science can predict who will turn out to be a mass murderer
    e. mass murderers are more "crazy than evil"

14. _____-oriented killers are murderers who are motivated to rid the world of a particular type of undesirable person.
    a. Mission
    b. Empirical
    c. Hedonistic
    d. Power
    e. Control

15. According to Keeney and Heide, which of the following is <u>true</u> about female serial killers:
    a. less than five percent of serial killers are women
    b. females were much more likely than males to use extreme violence and torture
    c. female killers tracked or stalked their victims
    d. women were more likely than men to poison their victims
    e. none of the above ("a" thru "d")

16. Which of the following is <u>true</u> about assault rates:
    a. highest in urban areas
    b. highest during the spring months
    c. highest in western regions
    d. all of the above ("a" thru "c")
    e. none of the above ("a" thru "c")

17. This type of robber steals to obtain small amounts of money when an accessible and vulnerable target presents itself.
    a. addict robber
    b. alcoholic robber
    c. professional robber
    d. opportunist robber

18. _____ terrorism is designed to promote the interests of a minority ethnic or religious group who have suffered under majority rule.
    a. Cultural
    b. Political
    c. Nationalistic
    d. Revolutionary

19. Which of the following is <u>true</u> about terrorism or terrorists:
    a. international terrorist groups are much less active than intranational groups in the United States
    b. the locus of most international terrorism is in eastern Europe
    c. terrorism requires violence without guilt
    d. terrorists tend to come from lower-class backgrounds

20. The most extreme form of state-sponsored terrorism:
    a. genocide
    b. ethnocide
    c. death squads
    d. massacres

21. Which of the following is not a common precipitant to workplace violence:
    a. economic restructuring
    b. leadership styles
    c. poor service
    d. romantic slights
    e. sympathetic managers

106

MATCHING

____	1.	Thanatos
____	2.	Hate crime
____	3.	Wolfgang & Ferracuti
____	4.	Feudal law
____	5.	Common law of rape
____	6.	Drug ingestion
____	7.	Terrorist
____	8.	Stranger violence
____	9.	Gang killings
____	10.	Romantic triangle
____	11.	Visionary killers
____	12.	Street robbery

A. Economic compulsive behavior
B. Instrumental
C. "Heiress stealing"
D. Response to inner voice
E. Death instinct
F. Mugging or yoking
G. Guerilla
H. Gay bashing
I. Corroboration
J. Drive by shootings
K. Expressive violence
L. Subculture of violence

ESSAY QUESTIONS

1. What is the possible role of human instinct in violent behavior?

2. Define the concept of subculture of violence.

3. What is the relationship between geography and culture of violence?

4. What is the history of rape?

5. Describe the biological, subcultural, and psychological explanations for rape.

6. Who is the rapist?

7. Explain the legal problems associated with rape. What remedies have been developed?

8. Describe the nature and extent of murder.

9. How important are victim-precipitated criminal homicides?

10. Under what circumstances do stranger homicides occur?

11. Identify and describe the four types of serial killers as defined by Ronald Holmes and James De Burger.

12. What are the causes of child abuse?

13. Identify and describe John Conklin's four types of robbers.

14. Why do people commit bias crimes?

15. Compare and contrast terrorism in the past to terrorism since the 1960s.

16. Identify and describe four forms of terrorism.

17.   Who is the terrorist?

18.   What factors contribute to workplace violence.

19.   Discuss how structural violence is a form of state-sponsored terrorism.

CHAPTER ELEVEN ANSWER SECTION

FILL-IN REVIEW

1.	subcultures		12.	Deliberation
2.	instinctual		13.	Felony
3.	Thanatos		14.	Thrill
4.	disputatiousness		15.	mass
5.	virility		16.	aggravated
6.	consent		17.	Child abuse
7.	shield		18.	robbery
8.	exemption		19.	Hate
9.	statute		20.	terrorism
10.	malice		21.	death
11.	Premeditation			

TRUE/FALSE

1.	F	14.	T
2.	F	15.	T
3.	T	16.	T
4.	F	17.	F
5.	F	18.	T
6.	T	19.	T
7.	T	20.	F
8.	T	21.	F
9.	T	22.	T
10.	F	23.	T
11.	F	24.	T
12.	T	25.	F
13.	F		

MULTIPLE CHOICE

1.	b	12.	b
2.	d	13.	b
3.	a	14.	a
4.	c	15.	d
5.	b	16.	a
6.	e	17.	d
7.	d	18.	c
8.	a	19.	c
9.	c	20.	a
10.	a	21.	e
11.	d		

MATCHING

1.	E
2.	H
3.	L
4.	C
5.	I
6.	A
7.	G
8.	B
9.	J
10.	K
11.	D
12.	F

12 Property Crimes

LEARNING OBJECTIVES

1. Define economic crimes.

2. Compare and contrast occasional criminals to professional criminals.

3. Describe what is known about the lives of professional criminals.

4. Describe the qualities of a successful professional fence.

5. Identify the various types of nonprofessional fences.

6. Describe the role of private justice in combatting shoplifting.

7. Describe what is known about naive check forgers and auto thieves.

8. Describe the evolving legal definition of burglary.

9. Explain the career of successful burglars.

10. Differentiate between male and female burglars.

11. Compare juvenile arsonists to business people involved in arson.

KEY TERMS AND CONCEPTS

Economic crimes
Fence
Street crimes
Burglary
Flash houses
Occasional criminals
Professional criminals
Situational inducements
Receivers
Fencing
Associational fences
Underground economy
Neighborhood hustlers
Amateur receivers
Larceny/theft
Constructive possession
Shoplifting
Five-finger discount
Boosters
Heels

Target removal
Target hardening
Bad checks
Naive check forgers
Closure
Systematic forgers
Credit card theft
Auto theft
Carjacking
False pretenses
Fraud
Confidence games
Pigeon drop
Embezzlement
Good burglar
Arson
Arson for profit
Arson fraud
Flashover

110

NAMES TO KNOW

John Hepburn	Ramiro Martinez, Jr.
Edwin Sutherland	Edwin Lemert
Carl Klockars	Charles McCaghy
Darrell Steffensmeier	Ronald Clarke
Marilyn Walsh	Patricia Harris
Paul Cromwell	Francis Hoheimer
James Olson	Richard Wright
D'Aunn Avary	Scott Decker
Mary Owen Cameron	Neal Shover
Donald Hartmann	Graham Farrell
Erhard Blankenburg	Coretta Phillips
Melissa Davis	Ken Pease
Richard Lundman	Wayne Wooden

FILL-IN REVIEW

1. The _____ is a buyer and seller of stolen merchandise.

2. _____ involves forcible entry into a home or place of work for the purpose of theft.

3. _____ criminals do not define themselves by a criminal role or view themselves as committed career criminals.

4. By the eighteenth century, city thieves congregated in _____ houses--public meeting places, often taverns, that served as headquarters for gangs.

5. During the eighteenth century _____ moved freely in sparsely populated areas and transported goods without bothering to pay tax or duty.

6. _____ lived in the country and supplemented their diet and income with game that belonged to a landlord in the eighteenth century.

7. At common law, _____ was defined as "the trespassory taking and carrying away of the personal property of another with intent to steal."

8. To get around the element of "trespass in the taking," English judges created the concept of _____ possession.

9. _____ is a common form of theft involving the taking of goods from retail stores.

10. Sometimes called _____ or heels, professional shoplifters intend to resell stolen merchandise to pawnshops or fences, usually at half the original prices.

11. According to Cameron's study of shoplifters, _____ are usually respectable persons who don't conceive of themselves as thieves.

12. Lemert found that the majority of check forgers--he calls them _____ check forgers-- are amateurs who don't believe their actions will hurt anyone.

13. Lemert found that a few professional check forgers--whom he calls _____ forgers-- make a substantial living by passing bad checks.

14. Auto theft is usually considered the pastime of relatively affluent, white, middle-class teenagers looking for excitement through _____.

15. False pretenses, or _____, involves a wrongdoer's misrepresenting a fact to cause a victim to willingly give his or her property to the wrongdoer, who keeps it.

16. _____ games are run by swindlers whose goal is to separate a victim (or sucker) from his or her hard-earned money.

17. In the _____ drop, a package or wallet containing money is "found" by a con man or woman.

18. At common law the crime of _____ is defined as "the breaking and entering of a dwelling house of another in the nighttime with the intent to commit a felony within."

21. The _____ firesetter sets fire to school property or surrounding areas in order to retaliate for some slight experienced at school.

22. A _____ burglar is a characterization applied by professional burglars to colleagues who have distinguished themselves as burglars.

TRUE/FALSE

1. Average citizens view violent crimes with a great deal more ambivalence than economic crimes.

2. Criminologists suspect that the great majority of economic crimes are the work of amateur criminals.

3. Situational inducements are long-term influences on a person's behavior that increase risk taking over time.

4. Much is known about the career patterns of professional thieves.

5. Most criminologists would consider drug addicts who steal to support their habit as professionals.

6. A significant portion of all fencing is performed by "amateur" or occasional criminals.

7. Klockars' work strongly suggests that fences customarily cheat their thief-clients and at the same time cooperate with the law.

8. Fences never engage in violence.

9. It seems likely that the fence is much less willing to cooperate with authorities than most other professional criminals.

10. During the fifteenth century, poachers moved freely in sparsely populated areas and transported goods without bothering to pay tax or duty.

112

11.	When a person misplaces his wallet and someone else finds it and keeps it--although identification of the owner can be plainly seen--the concept of constructive possession makes the person who has kept the wallet guilty of larceny.

12.	"Associational fences" buy and sell stolen property as but one of many ways they make a living.

13.	Cameron found that heels are usually respectable persons who don't conceive of themselves as thieves.

14.	Usually boosters who are arrested are first offenders who have never been apprehended before.

15.	One major problem associated with combatting shoplifting is that many customers who observe pilferage are reluctant to report it to security agents.

16.	In general, criminologists view shoplifters as people who are likely to reform if apprehended.

17.	Most credit card abuse is the work of professionals.

18.	Auto theft is one of the most highly reported of all major crimes.

19.	The mere act of moving property without the owner's consent, or damaging it, or using it, is considered embezzlement.

20.	The opportunity to become a good burglar is open to everyone.

21.	Burglary is one of the few crimes which has not increased substantially since 1985.

22.	According to Davis and her associates, a private justice system works in opposition to the public justice system when investigating shoplifting cases.

23.	There is much evidence which suggests that most arsons are psycho-sexually motivated.

MULTIPLE CHOICE

1.	_____ criminals do not define themselves by a criminal role or view themselves as committed career criminals.
	a.	Transitory
	b.	Occasional
	c.	Episodic
	d.	One-shot

2.	Professional offenders:
	a.	employ elaborate rationalizations to excuse the harmfulness of their actions
	b.	delude themselves with the belief that their acts are impulsive
	c.	attempt to learn from older criminals
	d.	all of the above ("a" thru "c")
	e.	none of the above ("a" thru "c")

3. Which of the following is a term for a shoplifter:
    a. Cannon
    b. Booster
    c. Sole
    d. Pennyweighter
    e. Prowl artist

4. A professional thief according to Conwell and Sutherland:
    a. engages in a variety of criminal acts
    b. depends solely on his wit and skill
    c. must have manual dexterity
    d. all of the above ("a" thru "c")
    e. none of the above ("a" thru "c")

5. Which of the following is <u>true</u> about private justice:
    a. 28 states have laws that allow stores to recover civil damages from shoplifters
    b. private security officers have few law enforcement powers
    c. the availability of civil damages has had little effect on decision making
    d. all of the above ("a" thru "c")
    e. none of the above ("a" thru "c")

6. Which of the following is <u>true</u> about female burglars:
    a. many female burglars also engaged in auto theft
    b. females always worked with a partner
    c. targets were chosen close to where the females lived
    d. all of the above ("a" thru "c")
    e. none of the above ("a" thru "c")

7. Wayne Wooden studied juvenile arsonists and found that they can be classified as:
    a. the "Playing with Matches" Firesetter
    b. the "Crying for Help" Firesetter
    c. the "Severely Disturbed" Firesetter
    d. all of the above ("a" thru "c")
    e. none of the above ("a" thru "c")

8. According to Sam Goodman, the fence studied by Darrell Steffensmeier, a fence must have:
    a. upfront cash
    b. knowledge of dealing
    c. complicity with law enforcers
    d. all of the above ("a" thru "c")
    e. none of the above ("a" thru "c")

9. Which of the following is <u>true</u> about larceny:
    a. most state jurisdictions have taken the common-law crime of larceny out of their legal codes
    b. as originally construed, larceny involved only taking property that was in the possession of the rightful owners
    c. the original definition of larceny included crimes in which the thief had come into the possession of the stolen property by trickery or deceit
    d. all of the above ("a" thru "c")
    e. none of the above ("a" thru "c")

10. Which of the following is <u>true</u> about naive check forgers:
    a. the majority are professionals
    b. most come from lower-class backgrounds
    c. most have strong identification with a criminal subculture
    d. they are often socially isolated people
    e. none of the above ("a" thru "d")

11. Usually older than joyriders and from a lower-class background, these auto thieves may repaint and otherwise disguise cars to avoid detection. They are part of the auto theft transaction category called:
    a. commission of another crime
    b. profit
    c. long-term transportation
    d. short-term transportation
    e. none of the above ("a" thru "d")

12. Which of the following is <u>true</u> about false pretenses:
    a. the definition of false pretenses was created by Congress after the Civil War to cover an area of law left untouched by fraud statutes
    b. false pretenses is similar to traditional larceny because the victims unwittingly give their possessions to the offender
    c. the crime does not involve a "trespass in the taking"
    d. all of the above ("a" thru "c")
    e. none of the above ("a" thru "c")

13. Which of the following is <u>true</u> about burglary:
    a. burglary is considered a less serious crime than larceny
    b. most jurisdictions punish burglary as a gross misdemeanor
    c. early laws against burglary were designed to protect a family whose home might be set upon by wandering criminals
    d. in recent years, most state jurisdictions have retained the necessity of forced entry in the definition of burglary
    e. none of the above ("a" thru "d")

14. Which of the following is <u>true</u> about careers in burglary:
    a. great variety exists within the ranks of burglars
    b. a star burglar is a characterization applied by amateur burglars to professionals who have distinguished themselves as burglars
    c. the star burglar must be able to work alone
    d. all of the above ("a" thru "c")
    e. none of the above ("a" thru "c")

15. Which of the following is a subclass of burglary:
    a. forcible entry
    b. unlawful entry where no force is used
    c. attempted forcible entry
    d. all of the above ("a" thru "c")
    e. none of the above ("a" thru "c")

16.   According to the NCVS, those most likely to be burglarized are:
   a.   southern upper class families
   b.   Hispanic and African-American families
   c.   college educated families
   d.   single-family residents
   e.   owner-occupied residents

17.   Arson is:
   a.   a crime committed primarily by males
   b.   a crime committed primarily by members of minority groups
   c.   a crime committed by middle aged persons
   d.   all of the above ("a" thru "c")
   e.   none of the above ("a" thru "c")

18.   Over the years, investigators have found that business people are willing to become involved in arson to:
   a.   collect fire insurance
   b.   take advantage of government funds available for redevelopment
   c.   solve labor-management problems
   d.   all of the above ("a" thru "c")
   e.   none of the above ("a" thru "c")

MATCHING

____	1. Fence	A.	"Five-finger discount"
____	2. Occasional property crime	B.	Fence acts as an informer
____	3. Edwin Sutherland	C.	Journeyman
____	4. Operation HEAT	D.	Buyer of stolen merchandise
____	5. Darrell Steffensmeier	E.	Combatting auto theft
____	6. Jack Wild	F.	"Accomplices" and "partners"
____	7. Grand larceny	G.	Situational inducement
____	8. Shoplifting	H.	Felony
____	9. Confidence game	I.	Technical competence
____	10. Burglary "career ladder"	J.	The Professional Thief
____	11. Females burglars	K.	Pigeon drop
____	12. Good burglars	L.	"Thief-Taker General..."

ESSAY QUESTIONS

1.   Why are people tolerant of economic crimes?

2.   Under what circumstances do occasional property crimes occur?

3.   Compare occasional offenders to professional criminals.

4.   Describe the career patterns of professional thieves.

5.   What are the critical dimensions of the professional theft according to Conwell and Sutherland?

116

6.   Compare the different types of occasional fences.

7.   Describe the life and times of a successful fence. What conditions must a fence meet to be successful?

8.   Identify and describe three separate groups of property criminals who were active by the eighteenth century.

9.   How does the crime of larceny differ today from the past?

10.   How is shoplifting controlled through private justice?

11.   What are the characteristics of the naive check forger?

12.   Identify and describe the five categories of auto theft transactions.

13.   Define burglary. Describe careers in burglary. What are the characteristics of the "good burglar?"

14.   Describe the similarities and differences between male and female burglars.

15.   How has technology influenced efforts to control shoplifting?

CHAPTER TWELVE ANSWER SECTION

FILL-IN REVIEW

1.	fence	11.	snitches
2.	Burglary	12.	naive
3.	Occasional	13.	systematic
4.	flash	14.	joyriding
5.	smugglers	15.	fraud
6.	Poachers	16.	Confidence
7.	larceny	17.	pigeon
8.	constructive	18.	burglary
9.	Shoplifting	19.	"Delinquent"
10.	boosters	20.	good

TRUE/FALSE

1.	F	13.	F
2.	T	14.	F
3.	F	15.	T
4.	F	16.	T
5.	F	17.	F
6.	T	18.	T
7.	T	19.	F
8.	T	20.	F
9.	F	21.	T
10.	F	22.	F
11.	T	23.	F
12.	F		

MULTIPLE CHOICE

1.	b	10.	d
2.	c	11.	c
3.	b	12.	c
4.	b	13.	c
5.	a	14.	a
6.	b	15.	d
7.	d	16.	b
8.	d	17.	a
9.	b	18.	d

MATCHING

1.	D
2.	G
3.	J
4.	E
5.	B
6.	L
7.	H
8.	A
9.	K
10.	C
11.	F
12.	I

13 White Collar and Organized Crime

LEARNING OBJECTIVES

1.   Define the evolving concept of white-collar crime.

2.   Explain the nature of white-collar crime in other countries.

3.   Identify and describe the characteristics of swindles and chiseling.

4.   Describe the activities of those individuals who exploit their power or position in organizations to take advantage of other individuals who have an interest in how that power is used.

5.   Explain and describe the different types of important corporate crimes.

6.   Explain the causes of white-collar crime from both the corporate culture and self-control viewpoints.

7.   Explain the two types of enforcement strategies--compliance and deterrence--used to control organizational deviance.

8.   Describe prosecution efforts toward white-collar crime on the federal, state and local levels.

9.   Evaluate how well white-collar criminals are punished.

10.   Describe the characteristics and activities of organized crime.

11.   Explain the relationships between organized crime and legitimate enterprises.

12.   Explain the meaning and value of the Racketeer Influenced and Corrupt Organization Act (RICO).

KEY TERMS AND CONCEPTS

Entrepreneurship	Influence peddling	Corporate culture theory
White collar crime	Bribery	Compliance
Organized crime	Accountability system	Laundering
Enterprise	Pilferage	Alien conspiracy theory
State-corporate crime	Reciprocal lending	Mafia
Stings	Desperation dealing	La Cosa Nostra
Swindles	Corporate/ organizational crime	Urban social bandits
Chiseling	Muckrakers	Yakuza
Short-weighting	Illegal restraint of trade	Racketeer influenced and corrupt
Securities fraud	Price fixing	organization act
Churning	Environmental crimes	Forfeiture
Insider trading	Virus	Zero tolerance
Arbitrage	Hacker	

NAMES TO KNOW

Dwight Smith
Mark Haller
Edwin Sutherland
Herbert Edelhertz
Ronald Kramer
Raymond Michalowski
Laura Schrager
James Short
Nikos Passas
David Nelken
Marshall Clinard
Richard Quinney
Mark Moore
John Clark
Richard Hollinger

Kitty Calavita
Robert Tillman
E. A. Ross
Michael Maltz
Stephen Pollack
Kathleen Daly
Donald Cressey
John Braithwaite
Travis Hirschi
Michael Gottfredson
Ellen Chayet
Elin Waring
Michael Benson
Elizabeth Moore

Paul Jesilow
Henry Pontell
Gilbert Geis
Peter Yeager
Michael Benson
Francis Cullen
William Maakestad
David Weisburd
Merry Morash
Philip Jenkins
Gary Potter
Alan Block
George Vold
Jay Albanese

FILL-IN REVIEW

1. _____ crime involves the <u>illegal</u> activities of people and institutions whose acknowledged purpose is profit and gain through <u>legitimate</u> business transactions.

2. A type of white-collar crime which includes antitrust violations, price-fixing, and false advertising is known as _____ crime.

3. According to Kramer and Michalowski, _____ crime is illegal or socially injurious actions resulting from cooperation between governmental and corporate institutions.

4. The collapse of the Bank of Credit and Commerce International is an example of a _____ which has cost depositors billions of dollars.

5. _____ involves cheating consumers on a regular basis such as charging for bogus auto repairs, cheating customers on home repairs, etc.

6. The _____ of a client's account by an unscrupulous stockbroker involves repeated, excessive, and unnecessary buying and selling of a stock.

7. Blue-collar employees have been involved in systematic theft of company property, commonly called _____.

8. The _____ horse is a technique in which one computer is used to reprogram another for illicit purposes.

9. A _____ is a program that disrupts or destroys existing programs and networks.

10. The _____ Commission found that a relatively small number of rogue cops were immersed in a pattern of violence, coercion, theft, and drug dealing.

11. In recent years, the definition of _____ _____ has been expanded by federal courts to include employees of financial institutions, such as law or banking firms, who misappropriate confidential information on pending corporate actions to purchase stock or give the information to a third party so that party may buy shares in the company.

12. _____ speculate on the stock of companies that are rumored to be takeover targets by other firms and hope to make profit on the difference between current stock prices and the price the acquiring company is willing to pay.

13. According to the Clean Water Act, a _____ is any "man-made or man-induced alteration of the chemical, physical, biological, and radiological integrity of the water."

14. According to the corporate _____ view, some business enterprises cause crime by placing excessive demands on employees while at the same time maintaining a business climate tolerant of employee deviance.

15. Hirschi and Gottfredson argue that white-collar criminals are people with low _____ who are inclined to follow momentary impulses without consideration of the long-term costs of such behavior.

16. _____ strategies aim for law conformity without the necessity of detecting, processing, or penalizing violators.

17. With _____ crime, a structured enterprise system is set up to supply consumers on a continuing basis with merchandise and services banned by the existing criminal law but for which a ready market exists.

18. A major premise of the _____ conspiracy theory is that the Mafia is centrally coordinated by a national committee that settles disputes, dictates policy, and assigns territory.

19. The _____ Committee, formed to look into organized crime, reported the existence of a national crime cartel whose members cooperated to make a profit and engaged in joint ventures to eliminate enemies.

20. _____ did not create new categories of crimes, but it did create new categories of offenses in racketeering activity, which it defined as involvement in two or more acts prohibited by 24 existing federal and 8 state statutes.

21. _____ is government seizure of property derived from or used in criminal activity.

TRUE/FALSE

1. Organized crime and white-collar crime are linked together because enterprise and not crime is the governing characteristic of both phenomena.

2. Sutherland's major concern was the crimes of middle class merchants.

3. According to Gilbert Geis, white-collar crimes can be committed by persons in all social classes.

4. A national survey of crime seriousness found that people saw a person stabbing another with a knife as being more serious than a doctor cheating on Medicare forms.

5. White collar crime in other countries is limited to official corruption.

6. White-collar swindlers, if caught, are usually charged with common-law crimes such as embezzlement or fraud.

7. It is uncommon for professionals to use their positions to chisel clients.

8. Blue-collar workers are the only employees who commit corporate theft.

9. Computer-related thefts are a new trend in employee theft and embezzlement.

10. In recent years, the state and federal governments have been vigorous in their prosecution of Medicaid fraud.

11. In tax evasion cases, a minimum dollar amount of fraud must exist before the government is authorized by law to take action.

12. Influence peddlers and bribe takers use their institutional position to grant favors and sell information to which their co-conspirators are not entitled.

13. Bribes are tax-deductible in Germany.

14. Deceptive pricing occurs when contractors provide the government or other corporations with incomplete or misleading information on how much it will actually cost to fulfill the contract they are bidding on or use mischarges once the contracts are signed.

15. Listerine mouthwash prevents the common cold.

16. Criminal penalties for false claims are frequently given.

17. According to Cressey, embezzlement is caused by what he calls a "nonshareable financial problem."

18. Compliance strategies reinforce stigmatizing and "shaming" businesspeople by focusing on the actor, rather than the act, in white-collar crime.

19. Most organized crime income comes from narcotics distribution, loansharking, and prostitution.

20. Most experts now agree that it is accurate to view organized crime in the United States as a national syndicate that controls all illegitimate rackets in an orderly fashion.

21. Drug dealing gangs dominate organized crime in Japan.

22. The federal and state governments actually did little to combat organized crime until fairly recently.

122

MULTIPLE CHOICE

1. The victims of white-collar crime can be:
   a. the general public
   b. the organization that employs the offender
   c. another competing organization
   d. all of the above ("a" thru "c")
   e. none of the above ("a" thru "c")

2. Herbert Edelhertz divides white-collar criminality into four distinct categories. An example of his category of collateral business crimes is:
   a. welfare fraud
   b. embezzlement
   c. use of false weights and measures
   d. fraudulent land sales
   e. tax cheating

3. In their study of workplace theft, John Clark and Richard Hollinger found that about _____ percent of employees reported involvement in pilferage.
   a. 15
   b. 35
   c. 55
   d. 65
   e. 85

4. A category of computer crimes:
   a. theft of services
   b. use of data in a computer system for personal gain
   c. unauthorized use of computers employed for various types of financial processing to obtain assets
   d. theft of property by computer for personal use or conversion to profit
   e. all of the above are categories of computer crimes ("a" thru "d")

5. With the _____ _____, an employee sets up a dummy account in the company's computerized records. A small amount---even a few pennies---is subtracted from customers' accounts and added to the account of the thief.
   a. impersonation mode
   b. data leakage
   c. logic bomb
   d. super zapping
   e. salami slice

6. The most widely publicized incident of government bribery in recent years was the _____ case.
   a. RICOSCAM
   b. PIMPSCAM
   c. HEWSCAM
   d. ABSCAM
   e. PROFSCAM

7.   The federal watchdog agency which attempts to control Wall Street activities:
      a.   The Bureau of Standards and Practices
      b.   The Agency for Business Equities
      c.   The Federal Bureau of Investigation
      d.   The Securities and Exchange Commission
      e.   The Commission to Investigate Corrupt Practices

8.   A type of white-collar crime which involves situations in which powerful institutions or their representatives willfully violate the laws that restrain these institutions from doing social harm or require them to do social good:
      a.   client frauds
      b.   influence peddling
      c.   corporate crime
      d.   securities violation
      e.   none of the above ("a" thru "d")

9.   The _____ _____ Act outlaws conspiracies between corporations designed to control the marketplace.
      a.   Securities Exchange
      b.   Sherman Antitrust
      c.   Exchange Business
      d.   Kefauver Reform
      e.   Business Practices

10.   A market condition that is considered so inherently anticompetitive that federal courts have defined it as illegal per se:
      a.   consolidation of the marketplace
      b.   freezing strikes
      c.   group boycotts
      d.   both "a" and "b" are relevant market conditions
      e.   both "a" and "c" are relevant market conditions

11.   _____ market sharing involves dividing the potential market into territories within which only one member of the conspiring group is permitted a low bid.
      a.   Identical
      b.   Geographical
      c.   Rotational
      d.   Predation
      e.   Volatile

12.   The control of workers' safety has been the province of:
      a.   OSHA
      b.   FTC
      c.   WCJEA
      d.   EPA
      e.   PCB

13. Federal response(s) to control environmental crimes:
    a. Toxic Substance Control Act
    b. Resource Conservation and Recovery Act of 1976
    c. Rivers and Harbors Act of 1899
    d. none of the above ("a" thru "c")
    e. all of the above ("a" thru "c")

14. According to corporate culture theory:
    a. illegal corporate behavior can only exist in secrecy
    b. public scrutiny fails to foster stigma since "everyone is doing it"
    c. the motives that produce white-collar crimes are the same as those that produce any other criminal behaviors
    d. both "a" and "b" are true
    e. both "a" and "c" are true

15. _____ strategies are the primary weapon against white-collar crime in the United States.
    a. Restitution
    b. Retribution
    c. Treatment
    d. Deterrence
    e. Compliance

16. On the state and local level:
    a. enforcement of white-collar laws is often organized and efficient
    b. evidence exists that local prosecutors will pursue white-collar criminals more vigorously if they are not distracted by the efforts of other law enforcement agencies
    c. research shows that local prosecutors did not consider white-collar crimes particularly serious problems
    d. all of the above ("a" thru "c")
    e. none of the above ("a" thru "c")

17. A survey of enforcement practices in nine states conducted by the federal government's Bureau of Justice Statistics found that:
    a. white-collar crimes account for about 22 percent of all arrest dispositions
    b. 18 percent of all those arrested for white-collar crimes were prosecuted
    c. 60 percent of white-collar criminals convicted in state court were incarcerated
    d. 72 percent of white-collar offenders received a prison term of more than two years
    e. none of the above ("a" thru "d") were findings

18. An organized crime feature:
    a. includes terrorists dedicated to political change
    b. employs predatory tactics
    c. activities are limited to providing illicit services
    d. is synonymous with the Mafia
    e. none of the above ("a" thru "d")

MATCHING

____	1.	Marketing techniques	A.	"Burglars in blue"
____	2.	Mafia crime family	B.	Economism
____	3.	State-corporate crime	C.	Chamber of Commerce
____	4.	Religious swindle	D.	Squander and liquidate
____	5.	S&L	E.	Threat, extortion
____	6.	Police corruption	F.	Predation
____	7.	Court system corruption	G.	Labor racketeering
____	8.	Price-fixing	H.	Ivan Boesky
____	9.	Arbitrage expert	I.	La Cosa Nostra
____	10.	Compliance systems	J.	Challenger explosion
____	11.	Alien conspiracy theory	K.	Operation Greylord
____	12.	McClellan Committee	L.	Jim Bakker

ESSAY QUESTIONS

1. In what ways can one link together organized crime and white-collar crime?

2. How did Edwin Sutherland view white-collar crime? How has the term been subsequently expanded?

3. How is white-collar crime more serious than street crimes?

4. What are the characteristics of white-collar crime in other countries?

5. Identify and describe Herbert Edelhertz's division of white-collar criminality into four distinct categories.

6. How do religious swindlers operate?

7. What groups are involved in chiseling?

8. Under what circumstances do individuals exploit their power or position in organizations to take advantage of other individuals who have an interest in how that power is used?

9. What are techniques used by employees to pilfer an organization?

10. What are common techniques used by computer criminals?

11. What is required to prove tax fraud?

12. What is one major difference that distinguishes influence peddling from exploitation of an institutional position?

13. What are examples of influence peddling in government, the criminal justice system, and business?

14. Explain the four types of market conditions that are considered so inherently anticompetitive that federal courts, through the Sherman Antitrust Act, have defined them as illegal per se.

126

15. What are types of environmental crimes? How has the federal government responded to environmental crimes?

16. How do corporate culture approaches explain white-collar crime?

17. Explain white-collar crime from a self-control framework.

18. What factors complicate white-collar crime enforcement?

19. What are the methods used in deterrence and compliance approaches to control white-collar crime?

20. How do state and local enforcement prosecutors respond to white-collar crime?

21. How severe is the punishment given to white-collar offenders as compared to other types of offenders?

22. What are the characteristics of organized crime?

23. What are the major activities of organized crime?

24. What is the relationship between organized crime and legitimate enterprises?

25. Explain the alien conspiracy theory. What are the problems with this theory?

26. How useful is RICO in controlling organized crime?

27. What has caused the decline in Mafia power?

CHAPTER THIRTEEN ANSWER SECTION

FILL-IN REVIEW

1.	White-collar		12.	Arbitragers
2.	corporate		13.	pollutant
3.	state-corporate		14.	culture
4.	swindle		15.	self-control
5.	Chiseling		16.	Compliance
6.	churning		17.	organized
7.	pilferage		18.	alien
8.	Trojan		19.	Kefauver
9.	virus		20.	RICO
10.	Mollen		21.	Forfeiture
11.	insider trading			

TRUE/FALSE

1.	T	13.	T
2.	F	14.	T
3.	T	15.	F
4.	F	16.	F
5.	F	17.	T
6.	T	18.	F
7.	F	19.	T
8.	F	20.	F
9.	T	21.	F
10.	F	22.	T
11.	F		
12.	T		

MULTIPLE CHOICE

1..	d	10.	c
2.	c	11.	b
3.	b	12.	a
4.	e	13.	e
5.	e	14.	a
6.	d	15.	d
7.	d	16.	c
8.	c	17.	c
9.	b	18.	b

MATCHING

1.	E
2.	C
3.	J
4.	L
5.	D
6.	A
7.	K
8.	F
9.	H
10.	B
11.	I
12.	G

14 Public Order Crimes

LEARNING OBJECTIVES

1. Explain the issues in the relationship between law and morality.

2. Describe societal and legal responses toward homosexuality, prostitution, and pornography.

3. Identify and describe the various types of prostitutes.

4. Describe the relationship between pornography and violence.

5. Identify and describe the most widely used illegal drugs.

6. Describe the nature and extent of substance abuse in the United States today.

7. Explain the relationship between drugs and crime.

8. Describe the laws that have been created to control drugs.

9. Evaluate the usefulness of each of the following drug control strategies: law enforcement, punishment, drug prevention, and treatment.

KEY TERMS AND CONCEPTS

Public order crime
Victimless crime
Dehumanized
Social harm
Vigilante
Moral crusade
Moral entrepreneur
Homosexuality
Sodomy
Homophobia
Paraphilia
Prostitution
Streetwalker

Hooker
Bar girls
Brothel prostitutes
Madams
Call girl
Call houses
Circuit travelers
Rap booth
Skeezer
Baby pro
Mann act
Pornography
Obscene

Temperance movement
Freebase
Crack
Designer drugs
Addiction-prone personality
Problem behavior syndrome
Smuggler
Occasional users
Stabilized junkies
Free-wheelers
Street junkies
DARE

NAMES TO KNOW

Andrea Dworkin
Morris Cohen
Sir Patrick Devlin
William O. Douglas
Alice Walker
H. L. A. Hart
Joseph Gussfield
Wayne LaFave
Austin Scott, Jr.
Daniel Claster
Albert Reiss
C. S. Ford
F. A. Beach

Paul Goldstein
Lisa Maher
Kathleen Daly
Jennifer James
Dorothy Bracey
Potter Stewart
Ann Wolbert Burgess
Berl Kutchinsky
Michael Goldstein
John Paul Stevens
Carrie Nation
Thomas Mieczkowski

Douglas Longshore
James Inciardi
Ruth Horowitz
Anne Pottieger
Claire Sterck-Elifson
Kenneth Tunnell
Karen Joe
M. Douglas Anglin
George Speckart
Charles Faupel
Carl Klockars
Saul Weingart

FILL-IN REVIEW

1. _____ order crimes involve acts that interfere with the operation of society and the ability of people to function efficiently.

2. From the Lone Ranger to Batman (the "Caped Crusader"), the righteous _____ is an accepted part of the general culture.

3. According to Howard Becker, moral _____ go on moral crusades to rid the world of evil.

4. Today, there are many reasons given for an extremely negative overreaction to homosexuals referred to as _____.

5. In the case of Robinson v. California, the U.S. Supreme Court determined that people could not be criminally prosecuted because of their _____ (for example, drug addict or homosexual).

6. A subset of masochistic behavior is hypoxphilia or _____ asphyxia, which by means of a noose, ligature, plastic bag, mask, volatile chemicals or chest compression a man or woman attempts partial asphyxia and oxygen deprivation to their brain, to enhance sexual gratification.

7. The _____, often a retired prostitute, was the senior administrator and owner of the brothel.

8. On the street women who barter drugs for sex are called _____.

9. Occasionally, but not as often as the media would like us to believe, pimps pick up young runaways, buy them clothes and jewelry, and turn them into _____ pros.

10. Often called the _____ _____ act, the Mann Act prohibits bringing women into the country or transporting them across state lines for the purposes of prostitution.

11. _____ is defined by Webster's dictionary as "deeply offensive to morality or decency...designed to incite to lust or depravity."

12.   The Attorney General's Commission on _____, set up by the Reagan administration to review the sale and distribution of sexually explicit material, concluded that many performers and models are the victims of physical and psychological coercion.

13.   The so-called _____ porn industry involves over a million children each year who are believed to be used in pornography or prostitution.

14.   In Pope v. Illinois, the U.S. Supreme Court articulated a _____ doctrine: a work is obscene if a reasonable person applying objective (national) standards would find the material lacking in any social value.

15.   General anesthetics act on the brain to produce a generalized loss of sensation, stupor, or unconsciousness (called _____).

16.   _____ are synthetic drugs that stimulate action in the central nervous system.

17.   _____ are drugs, either natural or synthetic, that produce vivid distortions of the senses without greatly disturbing the viewer's consciousness.

18.   _____ was first produced as a pain killing alternative to morphine in 1875 because it was considered non-addicting by its creator Heinrich Dreser (the name derives from the fact that it was considered a "hero" when first isolated).

19.   The Harrison Act of 1914 defined _____ as any drug that produces sleep and relieves pain, such as heroin, morphine, and opium.

20.   A major effort made to cut off drug supplies by destroying overseas crops and arresting members of drug cartels is known as _____ control.

21.   Border patrols and military personnel using sophisticated hardware have been involved in massive _____ efforts to control drug supplies.

22.   A _____ effect occurs when stepped-up efforts to curb drug dealing in one area or city simply encourages dealers to seek out friendlier "business" territory.

TRUE/FALSE

1.   Research on prostitution shows that few young runaway and abandoned children are coerced into a "life on the streets."

2.   It has long been the custom to ban or limit behaviors that are believed to run contrary to existing social norms, customs, and practices.

3.   Homosexuality is a disease that can be caught.

4.   To engage in homosexual behavior means one is a homosexual.

5.   Laws providing the death penalty for homosexuals existed until 1991 in France, until 1961 in England, and until 1989 in Scotland.

6.   No state allows same sex marriages.

7.   In a surprising move, voters in Cincinnati, Ohio passed a city ordinance in 1993 which banned discrimination in housing or employment based on sexual orientation.

8.   It is likely that the number of men who hire prostitutes is declining.

9.   Arrests for prostitution have increased dramatically in the past decade.

10.   Brothels declined in importance following World War II.

11.   Evidence exists that girls become prostitutes because of psychological problems or personality disturbances.

12.   Typically, prostitution is considered a misdemeanor.

13.   In 1970, the National Commission on Obscenity and Pornography found a strong relationship between pornography and violence.

14.   Experimental laboratory studies have found that men exposed to violence in pornography are more likely to act aggressively toward women.

15.   Sex for profit predates Western civilization.

16.   Amphetamines are probably the major cause of drug overdose deaths.

17.   Cocaine, or coke, is the most powerful natural stimulant.

18.   Crack is a new substance.

19.   Heroin today is the most commonly used narcotic in the United States.

20.   Prohibition turned out to be a success.

21.   According to the <u>Household Survey on Drug Abuse</u>, a dramatic increase in drug use occurred between 1985 and 1992.

22.   Intravenous drug users are the second largest risk group, after homosexual males, for HIV infection (HIV is the AIDS-causing virus).

23.   No state provides addicts with sterile needles.

24.   Research on the psychological characteristics of drug abusers does reveal the presence of a significant degree of personal pathology.

25.   The results of the first large-scale study on the personality characteristics of abusers indicate a lack of association between drug abuse and mental illness.

26.   What little is known about drug smugglers indicates they are generally young men, in their twenties, who have weak organizational skills, few solid connections, some capital to invest, and an aversion toward taking large business risks.

27.   Though women are just as likely as men to use drugs, female offenders are less likely to be involved in drugs than male offenders.

MULTIPLE CHOICE

1.   Which of the following is <u>true</u> about crime and morality:
    a.   It is a crime in most jurisdictions to ignore the pleas of a drowning person.
    b.   It is a crime to kill a loved one who is suffering from an incurable disease in order to spare them further pain.
    c.   A good motive will normally prevent what is otherwise criminal from being a crime.
    d.   all of the above is true ("a" thru "c")
    e.   none of the above is true ("a" thru "c")

2.   Homosexual behavior:
    a.   has existed in few societies
    b.   among males has been viewed as normal in 49 preliterate societies.
    c.   is engaged in exclusively by 29 percent of the male population according to estimates
    d.   both "b" and "c" are true about homosexual behavior
    e.   none of the above is true ("a" thru "c")

3.   A survey conducted by the Gallup organization found that _____ of the general public do not consider homosexuality an acceptable life-style.
    a.   fewer than one percent
    b.   ten percent
    c.   more than half
    d.   three quarters
    e.   ninety percent

4.   In 1986, the Supreme Court in _____ _____ upheld a Georgia statute making it a crime to engage in consensual sodomy.
    a.   <u>Bowers v. Hardwick</u>
    b.   <u>Roth v. United States</u>
    c.   <u>Powell v. Texas</u>
    d.   <u>Ingraham v. Wright</u>
    e.   <u>Buck v. Bell</u>

5.   About _____ states have decriminalized private, consensual sodomy between adult homosexuals.
    a.   six
    b.   eleven
    c.   sixteen
    d.   twenty
    e.   thirty

6.   Homosexuals:
    a.   were not allowed to join the FBI until 1993
    b.   may not be evicted from private housing at the landlord's discretion
    c.   are not prohibited from living together in public housing projects
    d.   all of the above are true ("a" thru "c")

7. An outlawed sexual behavior involving the rubbing against or touching of a nonconsenting person in a crowd, elevator, or other public area is called _____.
   a. paraphilias
   b. frotteurism
   c. pedophilia
   d. rubberism
   e. none of the above ("a" thru "d")

8. The aristocrats of prostitution:
   a. B-girls
   b. madams
   c. circuit travelers
   d. rap booth prostitutes
   e. call girls

9. Prostitution is currently illegal in all states except:
   a. New York
   b. New Mexico
   c. Arizona
   d. Washington
   e. Nevada

10. _____ rings have well-structured organizations that recruit children and create extensive networks of customers who desire sexual services.
    a. Syndicated
    b. Transition
    c. Solo
    d. Linear
    e. Enterprise

11. The _____ Amendment of the U.S. Constitution protects free speech and prohibits police agencies from limiting the public's right of free expression.
    a. First
    b. Fourth
    c. Sixth
    d. Ninth
    e. Fourteenth

12. To convict a person of obscenity under the _____ doctrine, the state or local jurisdiction must specifically define obscene conduct in its statute, and the pornographer must engage in that behavior.
    a. Robinson
    b. Ferber
    c. Mapplethorpe
    d. Cardinal
    e. Miller

13.   The most widely abused anesthetic drug is phencyclidine (PCP), known on the streets as

_____ _____.

    a.   "pcp pills"
    b.   "blue dragons"
    c.   "goof balling"
    d.   "angel dust"
    e.   "benny dex"

14.   _____ is a chemical produced from street cocaine by treating it with a liquid to remove the hydrochloric acid with which pure cocaine is bonded during manufacture.
    a.   Basuco
    b.   Freebase
    c.   Methedrine
    d.   DMT
    e.   Alkaloid

15.   Heroin abuse is generally considered a(n) _____ phenomenon.
    a.   upper-class
    b.   lower-class
    c.   middle-class
    d.   all of the above ("a" thru "c")--a significant problem for all classes
    e.   none of the above ("a" thru "c")--a problem which is unrelated statistically to issues of social class

16.   According to Klockars and Faupel, if stable heroin users make a "big score," perhaps through a successful drug deal, they may significantly increase their drug use and become:
    a.   occasional users
    b.   stabilized junkies
    c.   free-wheelers
    d.   street junkies
    e.   none of the above ("a" thru "d")

17.   Which of the following is true about alcohol abuse:
    a.   nearly 500 people die in alcohol-related accidents and 20,000 are injured in an average week
    b.   judges in Quincy, Massachusetts have agreed to put every drunk-driving offender in jail for three days
    c.   treatment efforts to help chronic alcoholics have not proved successful
    d.   the Supreme Court ruled in Powell v. Texas that a chronic alcoholic could be convicted under state public drunkenness laws
    e.   all of the above is true ("a" thru "d")

18.   Adult predatory drug users who are rarely arrested:
    a.   bridge the gap between adult drug distributors and the adolescent user
    b.   are frequently related to gang members
    c.   have few skills
    d.   are known for their calculated violence
    e.   none of the above ("a" thru "d")

19.   Drug-involved youth who continue to commit crimes as adults:
    a.   have few other offenders in their family
    b.   came from working class families and did well while in school
    c.   started using drugs at a relatively young age
    d.   used few types of drugs
    e.   none of the above ("a" thru "d")

MATCHING

____	1.	Sodomy	A.	Transition rings
____	2.	Pedophilia	B.	"To the side of"
____	3.	Prostitution	C.	"To cause to stand in front of"
____	4.	Streetwalker	D.	Methadone
____	5.	Pimps	E.	Deviant intercourse
____	6.	Child pornography	F.	Drug Use Forecasting
____	7.	Opium	G.	Baby pros
____	8.	Greek para	H.	Prepubescent children
____	9.	Temperance movement	I.	DARE
____	10.	Drug prevention strategy	J.	Prohibition
____	11.	Drug treatment strategy	K.	"Plant of joy"
____	12.	Survey of known criminals	L.	Union General Hooker's army

ESSAY QUESTIONS

1.   Who defines morality?

2.   What is the relationship between law and morality?

3.   Compare Sir Patrick Devlin's views toward morality in the law to H.L.A. Hart's views toward legislating morals.

4.   What have been the attitudes toward homosexuality? How have laws attempted to control homosexuality?

5.   Describe the various types of prostitutes.

6.   What attracts men to the life of the pimp? How has the role of the pimp changed?

7.   What are some of the reasons for a woman turning to prostitution?

8.   What is the relationship between pornography and violence?

9.   What was the Supreme Court holding in its decision of Miller v. California?

10.   Describe the similarities and differences among anesthetics, barbiturates, tranquilizers, and amphetamines?

11.   Why did Prohibition fail?

136

12.   How extensive is the substance abuse problem today?

13.   Is drug use declining? Explain.

14.   Identify subcultural views for substance abuse.

15.   Identify psychodynamic views for substance abuse.

16.   What are the characteristics of adolescents who are involved in drugs either through distributing small amounts or frequently selling drugs?

17.   What are the characteristics of adult drug users who are either frequently or rarely arrested?

18.   Outline the relationship between drug use and crime.

19.   How useful are the laws created to control drunk driving?

20.   How successful have law enforcement and punishment efforts been in controlling drugs?

21.   Describe the problems with the argument for drug legalization.

CHAPTER FOURTEEN ANSWER SECTION

FILL-IN REVIEW

1.	Public	12.	Pornography
2.	vigilante	13.	kiddy
3.	entrepreneurs	14.	reasonableness
4.	homophobia	15.	narcosis
5.	status	16.	Amphetamines
6.	autoerotic	17.	Hallucinogens
7.	madam	18.	Heroin
8.	"skeezers"	19.	narcotics
9.	baby	20.	source
10.	white slave	21.	interdiction
11.	Obscenity	22.	displacement

TRUE/FALSE

1.	F	15.	T				
2.	T	16.	F				
3.	F	17.	T				
4.	F	18.	F				
5.	F	19.	T				
6.	T	20.	F				
7.	F	21.	F				
8.	T	22.	T				
9.	F	23.	F				
10.	T	24.	T				
11.	F	25.	F				
12.	T	26.	F				
13.	F	27.	F				
14.	T						

MULTIPLE CHOICE

1.	e	11.	a
2.	b	12.	e
3.	c	13.	d
4.	a	14.	b
5.	d	15.	b
6.	a	16.	c
7.	b	17.	e
8.	e	18.	d
9.	e	19.	c
10.	a		

MATCHING

1.	E
2.	H
3.	C
4.	L
5.	G
6.	A
7.	K
8.	B
9.	J
10.	I
11.	D
12.	F

15 Overview of the Criminal Justice System

LEARNING OBJECTIVES

1.   Define the concept of criminal justice.

2.   Describe the functions and roles of the police, courts, and corrections.

3.   Describe the similarities and differences between juvenile and adult justice systems.

4.   Identify and describe each of the major decision points in the processing of a felony offender.

5.   Describe the four layers of Walker's "wedding cake" model of criminal justice. Assess its usefulness.

6.   Explain the value of procedural laws in our society.

7.   Define the various dimensions of the concept of due process.

8.   Describe the meaning of and controversies about the exclusionary rule.

9.   Describe the meaning and importance of the six models of justice: crime control, justice, due process, rehabilitation, nonintervention and radical.

10.   Explain the role of the various philosophies of justice today.

KEY TERMS AND CONCEPTS

Depression-era outlaws	Complaint/charging	Due process
Criminal justice	Preliminary hearing	Bill of rights
Social control	Indictment	Exclusionary rule
Chicago crime commission	Arraignment	Good faith exception
Wickersham commission	Grand jury	Crime control model
Sheriff's departments	Fundamental fairness	Justice model
LEAA	Plea Bargaining	Determinate sentencing
Police	Bail	Rehabilitation model
Law Enforcement	Adjudication	Nonintervention model
Courts	Disposition	Deinstitutionalization
Corrections	Penitentiaries	Diversion
Juvenile justice	Parole	Decriminalization
Parens patriae	Lineup	Net widening
Initial contact	Probable cause	Radical model
Investigation	"Wedding Cake" model	Praxis
Arrest	Hands-off doctrine	Restorative Justice
Custody	Procedural laws	

NAMES TO KNOW

Herbert Hoover
Wayne LaFave
Donald Newman
Lyndon Johnson
Herbert Packer
Samuel Walker
Earl Warren
Warren Berger
William Rehnquist

Craig Uchida
Timothy Bynum
David Fogel
Paul Gendreau
Robert Ross
Edwin Lemert
Edwin Schur
Richard Quinney

FILL-IN REVIEW

1.   _____ _____ refers to both the formal process and the component agencies that have been established to apprehend, adjudicate, sanction, and treat criminal offenders.

2.   An _____ occurs when the police take a person into custody and deprive the person of freedom for allegedly committing a criminal act.

3.   In 1919 the _____ Crime Commission, a professional association funded by private contributions, was created to act as a citizens' advocate group and to keep track of the activities of local justice agencies.

4.   The _____ _____ is considered by many to be the core element in the administration of criminal justice.

5.   Under the Fifth and Fourteenth Amendments of the Constitution, the defendant has the right to be treated with _____ fairness.

6.   In the system of _____ _____, defendants are asked to plead guilty as charged in return for consideration of leniency or mercy.

7.   Following conviction and sentencing, the offender enters the _____ system.

8.   _____ is a legal disposition that allows the convicted offender to remain in the community, subject to conditions imposed by court order under the supervision of a state agent.

9.   State and federally operated facilities that receive felony offenders sentenced by the criminal courts are called prisons or _____.

10.   Most new inmates are first sent to a reception and _____ center, where they are given diagnostic evaluations and are assigned to institutions that meet individual needs as much as possible within the system's resources.

11.   _____ correctional facilities emphasize the use of small neighborhood residential centers, halfway houses, prerelease centers, and work-release and home-furlough programs.

12. _____ is a process whereby an inmate is selected for early release and serves the remainder of the sentence in the community under the supervision of a state agent.

13. When a person is taken to the police station to be fingerprinted and photographed and to have personal information recorded, the police are using a procedure that is popularly referred to as _____.

14. A _____ is a term that is used to refer to a procedure when witnesses are brought in to view the suspect.

15. Suspects may be interrogated by police officers to get their side of the story, they may be asked to sign a _____ of guilt, or they may be asked to identify others involved in the crime.

16. _____ are used in misdemeanors; informations and indictments are employed in felonies.

17. Since it is a tremendous personal and financial burden to stand trial for a serious felony crime, the U.S. Constitution provides that the state must first prove to an impartial hearing board that there is _____ _____ that the accused committed the crime, and therefore, that there is sufficient reason to try the person as charged.

18. In a _____ hearing or probable cause hearing, an information is filed before an impartial lower-court judge, who decides whether the case should go forward.

19. During an _____ defendants are apprised of the formal charges and informed of their constitutional rights, have their bail considered, and have the trial date set.

20. The _____ cake model is an intriguing alternative to the traditional criminal justice flow chart.

21. Most criminal justice experts view the process as being dominated by judges, prosecutors, and defense counsels who work in concert to get the job done; this spirit of cooperation is referred to as the courtroom _____ _____.

22. The _____ doctrine refers to a policy of U.S. courts to exercise little control over the operations of criminal justice agencies.

23. Under the concept of fundamental _____, if the Supreme Court decided that a particular guarantee in the Bill of Rights was fundamental to and implicit in the U.S. system of justice, it would hold that guarantee applicable to the states.

24. The concept of _____ _____ is mentioned in the Fifth and Fourteenth Amendments and is usually divided into both substantive and procedural areas.

25. The _____ _____ means that evidence judged to be improperly obtained by police through illegal interrogation of suspects or searches of their person and property cannot be used (or even mentioned) against them in a court of law. It is as if the evidence did not exist.

26.   Those espousing the _____ _____ model believe that the overriding purpose of the justice system is protection of the public, deterrence of criminal behavior, and incapacitation of known criminals.

27.   Noninterventionist philosophy was influenced by Edwin Lemert's call for _____ nonintervention and Edwin Schur's 1971 book, Radical Nonintervention.

28.   Noninterventionists advocated deinstitutionalization of nonserious offenders, diversion from formal court processes into informal treatment programs, and _____ of nonserious offenses, such as the possession of small amounts of marijuana.

29.   _____ the net refers to the process by which efforts to remove people from the justice system actually enmesh them further within it.

30.   A movement has developed to supplement the criminal justice system with _____ crime prevention programs in which citizens engage in neighborhood patrols, blocks watches, and other self-help programs.

TRUE/FALSE

1.   Only the criminal justice system maintains the power to control crime and punish criminals.

2.   Common criminal justice agencies have only existed for 50 years or so.

3.   The modern era of criminal justice study began in 1921 when the National Commission on Law Enforcement, appointed by President Harding, published its final report entitled the Wickersham Report.

4.   Approximately 2,000 law enforcement agencies are operating in the United States.

5.   Every state except Hawaii maintains a state police force.

6.   The police have traditionally been defensive toward and suspicious of the public, resistant to change, and secretive in their activities.

7.   "Bargain justice" is estimated to occur in less than 65 percent of all criminal trials.

8.   Today more than 12 million people are on probation, and more than 50 percent of felony offenders receive a probation sentence.

9.   A person given a sentence involving incarceration ordinarily is confined to a correctional institution for a specified period of time.

10.   Inmates receive reasonably good treatment at many short-term institutions such as jails principally because they are administered by local county governments, have personnel with high qualifications, and provide quality services.

11.   Parens Patriae means that the state is acting in the best interests of children in trouble who can not care for themselves.

12. A police officer is required to use the word <u>arrest</u> or a similar word to initiate an arrest.

13. The law allows suspects to have their lawyers present when police conduct in-custody interrogations.

14. Bail is a money bond.

15. Most incarcerated offenders are denied the opportunity for a short period of probation before the expiration of the maximum term given them by the court.

16. The Walker model is useful because it helps us realize that public opinion about criminal justice is often formed on the basis of what happened in a few celebrated cases.

17. The law of criminal procedure guarantees citizens certain rights and privileges when they are accused of crime.

18. The guarantees of freedom contained in the Bill of Rights initially applied only to the individual state governments and did not affect the federal government.

19. The elements and the definition of due process seem to be flexible and constantly changing.

20. In recent years the rights of both those accused of crime and those convicted of crime have been expanded.

21. The U.S. Supreme Court has ruled that convictions would not be automatically overturned even if it is shown that police officers used coercion to obtain confessions.

22. Studies indicate that exclusionary rule violations occur rather frequently.

23. The exclusionary rule is of great symbolic value.

24. The crime control philosophy has become a dominant force in U.S. justice.

25. More than 45 percent of Americans disapprove of capital punishment.

MULTIPLE CHOICE

1. Today, police, court, and correctional agencies are viewed as components in a large integrated _____ _____ _____ which manages law violators from the time of their arrest through trial, punishment, and release.
   a. "social defense process"
   b. "people processing system"
   c. "coercive control system"
   d. "management process mechanism"
   e. "social control process"

2.	The overwhelming majority of the separate agencies engaged in justice-related activities are part of _____ government structures.
	a.	transnational
	b.	federal
	c.	regional
	d.	state
	e.	local

3.	Depending on the jurisdiction, sheriff's departments:
	a.	provide police protection in the unincorporated areas of the county
	b.	perform judicial functions
	c.	maintain the county jail and detention facilities
	d.	all of the above ("a" thru "c")
	e.	none of the above ("a" thru "c")

4.	The most visible agents of the justice process:
	a.	judges
	b.	prosecutors
	c.	police
	d.	probation officers
	e.	lawyers

5.	The most common correctional treatment:
	a.	diversion
	b.	rehabilitation
	c.	incapacitation
	d.	compensation
	e.	probation

6.	A prison cell costs about _____ to construct.
	a.	$5,500
	b.	$18,500
	c.	$50,000
	d.	$70,000

7.	A difference between juvenile and adult justice systems:
	a.	the right to receive Miranda warnings applies to adults but not to juveniles
	b.	plea bargaining exists for adult offenders but not juvenile offenders
	c.	the standard of evidence in adult criminal trials is proof beyond a reasonable doubt while in juvenile proceedings the standard of proof is a preponderance of the evidence.
	d.	the standard of arrest is more stringent for adults than for juveniles

8.	In about half the states and in the federal system, the decision on whether to bring a suspect to trial (indictment) is made by a group of citizens brought together to form:
	a.	a preliminary hearing
	b.	an arraignment panel
	c.	an adjudication
	d.	a pretrial disposition hearing
	e.	a grand jury

9.   The _____ layer of the cake is made up of the millions of misdemeanors, such as disorderly conduct, shoplifting, public drunkenness, bad checks, and minor assault that are processed each year.
      a.   first
      b.   second
      c.   third
      d.   fourth
      e.   fifth

10.   People in the _____ layer of the criminal justice wedding cake receive a great deal of public attention and their cases usually involve the full panoply of criminal justice procedures.
      a.   first
      b.   second
      c.   third
      d.   fourth
      e.   fifth

11.   Which of the following is a finding of a leading constitutional case:
      a.   police need to tell suspects in custody about a call from their attorney (Moran v. Burbine [1986])
      b.   police need a warrant to search trash left at the curbside (California v. Greenwood [1988])
      c.   a confession may be used at trial even if police used coercion when it was acquired (Arizona v. Fulminate [1991])
      d.   all of the above ("a" thru "c") are findings of leading constitutional cases
      e.   none of the above ("a" thru "c") are findings of leading constitutional cases

12.   In 1868, the _____ Amendment made the first ten amendments to the Constitution binding on the state governments.
      a.   Twelfth
      b.   Fourteenth
      c.   Sixteenth
      d.   Nineteenth

13.   The _____ Amendment states that a person has the right to be represented by legal counsel at a criminal trial.
      a.   Second
      b.   Fourth
      c.   Sixth
      d.   Eighth

14.   Under the leadership of _____ _____, who became the Chief Justice of the U.S. Supreme Court in 1953, the due process movement reached its peak.
      a.   William Rehnquist
      b.   Clarence Thomas
      c.   Warren Burger
      d.   William Douglas
      e.   Earl Warren

15. The fairness doctrine as expressed in due process of the law is guaranteed under both the
_____ and Fourteenth Amendments.
   a. First
   b. Fourth
   c. Fifth
   d. Sixth
   e. Eighth

16. The primary function of the _____ Amendment is to protect the individual against an
illegal arrest and to prevent illegal searches and seizures of a person's possessions.
   a. First
   b. Fourth
   c. Fifth
   d. Sixth

17. The crime control model:
   a. was influenced by positivist criminology
   b. advocates dealing with the root causes of crime
   c. is consistent with the "medical model"
   d. has its roots in classical theory

18. Those who subscribe to the due process model believe in:
   a. increasing the size of police forces
   b. maximizing the use of discretion
   c. building more prisons
   d. individualized justice and treatment

19. The nonintervention model is consistent with:
   a. diversion
   b. institutionalization
   c. recriminalization
   d. the therapeutic state

20. Those who subscribe to the _____ model advocate flat or determinate sentencing
statutes:
   a. rehabilitation
   b. process
   c. nonintervention
   d. radical
   e. justice

146

MATCHING

____	21.	Radical model	A.	Probation
____	22.	Truants	B.	Deinstitutionalization
____	23.	Booking	C.	"House arrest"
____	24.	Complaints	D.	Praxis
____	25.	Informations	E.	Misdemeanors
____	26.	Computer surveillance	F.	Good faith exception
____	27.	Community supervision	G.	Capital punishment statute
____	28.	Chief Justice Earl Warren	H.	Status offenders
____	29.	Nonintervention model	I.	Felonies
____	30.	Substantive due process	J.	Notice of charges
____	31.	Procedural due process	K.	Hands-off doctrine lifted
____	32.	Exclusionary rule	L.	Photographed & fingerprinted

ESSAY QUESTIONS

1. How is criminal justice a "people-processing system?"

2. What are important roles and functions of the police, courts, and corrections?

3. What are five similarities and five differences between juvenile and adult justice systems?

4. What are the major decision points in the processing of a felony offender?

5. Is there a criminal justice wedding cake? Explain.

6. How important is the Fourteenth Amendment in understanding the applicability of the Bill of Rights to the states?

7. Compare substantive due process to procedural due process.

8. Should we retain the exclusionary rule? Explain.

9. Compare the similarities and differences between the crime control model and the justice model.

10. In what ways is the radical model useful?

11. What is the role today of non-traditional methods of punishment and correction?

CHAPTER FIFTEEN ANSWER SECTION

FILL-IN REVIEW

1.	Criminal justice	16.	Complaints
2.	arrest	17.	probable cause
3.	Chicago	18.	preliminary
4.	criminal court	19.	arraignment
5.	fundamental	20.	wedding
6.	plea bargaining	21.	work group
7.	correctional	22.	hands-off
8.	Probation	23.	fairness
9.	penitentiaries	24.	due process
10.	classification	25.	exclusionary rule
11.	Community-based	26.	crime control
12.	Parole	27.	judicious
13.	booking	28.	decriminalization
14.	lineup	29.	Widening
15.	confession	30.	community

TRUE/FALSE

1.	T	14.	T
2.	F	15.	F
3.	F	16.	T
4.	F	17.	T
5.	T	18.	F
6.	T	19.	T
7.	F	20.	F
8.	F	21.	T
9.	T	22.	F
10.	F	23.	T
11.	T	24.	T
12.	F	25.	F
13.	T		

MULTIPLE CHOICE

1.	b	11.	c
2.	e	12.	b
3.	d	13.	c
4.	c	14.	e
5.	e	15.	c
6.	d	16.	b
7.	d	17.	d
8.	e	18.	d
9.	d	19.	a
10.	a	20.	e

MATCHING

1.	D
2.	H
3.	L
4.	E
5.	I
6.	C
7.	A
8.	K
9.	B
10.	G
11.	J
12.	F

148

16 Police and Law Enforcement

LEARNING OBJECTIVES

1. Trace the history of the policing from its origins to the present.

2. Compare the functions of law enforcement agencies on the federal, state, county, and local levels.

3. Define and describe community, and problem-oriented policing.

4. Describe the functions of patrol and investigation and analyze their effectiveness.

5. Describe the meaning of custodial interrogation and the Supreme Court decision in the case of Miranda v. Arizona. List several guidelines that the Supreme Court has articulated in limiting the range of the Miranda warning.

6. Explain the rules governing the use of search warrants and warrantless searches.

7. Discuss the factors associated with developing the police personality.

8. Define and describe the exercise of police discretion.

9. Describe the problems experienced by female and black police officers.

10. Discuss the various factors that have been related to police violence.

11. Explain the mechanisms that have been employed to control deadly force.

12. Delineate the role of technology in improving police effectiveness.

KEY TERMS AND CONCEPTS

Gatekeepers
Mollen commission
Pledge system
Tithing
Hundred
Constable
Shire
Shire reeve
Watch system
Justice of the peace
Wickersham commission
Federal Bureau of Investigation
COINTELPRO

Sheriff
State police
Metropolitan police
Order maintenance
Peacekeeping
Community policing
Proactive policing
Reactive policing
Foot patrols
Neighborhood policing
Problem oriented policing
Crackdown
Hot spots
Blue curtain

Operation pressure point
Internal affairs division
Aggressive preventive patrol
Mug shots
Modus operandi
Sting
Custodial interrogation
Miranda warning
Search and seizure
Police personality
Selective enforcement
Deadly force
Inevitable discovery rule

NAMES TO KNOW

Edward I
Sir Robert Peel
Samuel Walker
Calvin Coolidge
Herbert Hoover
August Vollmer
O.W. Wilson
Richard J. Daley
J. Edgar Hoover
Martin Luther King
James Q. Wilson
George Kelling
Herman Goldstein
Lynn Zimmer
Roger Dunham
Geoffrey Alpert
Barbara Boland

Robert Sampson
Jacqueline Cohen
William Westly
Joseph Goldstein
David Klinger
Stephen Mastrofski
Ronald Weitzer
Cassia Spohn
Miriam DeLone
Robert Worden
Robin Shepard
Marvin Krohn
James Jacobs
Jay Cohen
Stephen Leinen
Alice Stebbins

Catherine Milton
Joanne Belknap
Jill Kastens Shelley
Susan Martin
Thurgood Marshall
Albert Reiss
Anthony Pate
Lorie Fridell
Kim Michelle Lersch
Tom Mieczkowski
James Fyfe
Peter Scharf
Arnold Binder
David Greenberg
Craig Uchida
Robert Goldberg

FILL-IN REVIEW

1. With the pledge system, people were grouped into a collective of ten families called a _____ and entrusted with policing their own minor problems.

2. The _____, who might be considered the first real police officer, dealt with more serious breaches of the law.

3. In the thirteenth century, during the reign of King Edward I, the _____ system was created to help protect property in England's larger cities and towns.

4. In 1829, Sir Robert _____, England's Home Secretary, guided through Parliament an "Act for Improving the Police In and Near the Metropolis."

5. The _____ Commission, created by President Herbert Hoover, studied police issues on a national scale and identified in its 1931 report many of the problems of policing including a weak command structure and overly complex job requirements.

6. The onset of police professionalism might be traced to the influence of August _____.

7. The county police department is an independent agency whose senior officer, the _____, is usually an elected political official.

8. The concept of _____ policing brought together groups of junior officers and a supervisor to take command over a designated neighborhood area on a twenty-four-hour-a-day basis.

9. In _____ policing, departments play an active role in identifying particular community problems---street level drug dealers, prostitution rings, gang hangouts---and develop strategies to counteract them.

150

10.   _____ entails police officers' visible presence on the streets and public places.

11.   In early police forces, each officer had a particular area, or _____, to walk.

12.   In some places, _____ preventive patrol, designed to suppress crime before it occurs, has heightened tensions between the police and the minority community.

13.   When patrol officers take inappropriate action, or when their behavior results in violence or death, they are subject to intense scrutiny by public agencies and may be subject to disciplinary measures from the police department's _____ _____ division.

14.   The most comprehensive effort to evaluate the patrol function, the _____ _____ study, found that police patrol had little effect on crime patterns.

15.   The _____ has been a figure of great romantic appeal since the first independent investigative bureau was established by the London Metropolitan Police in 1841.

16.   Police pose as fences and conduct property transactions with thieves interested in selling stolen merchandise in _____ type of operations.

17.   Information provided by a suspect that leads to the seizure of incriminating evidence is permissible if the evidence would have been obtained anyway by other means or sources; this is now referred to as the _____ discovery rule.

18.   A suspect can be questioned in the field without a _____ warning if the information the police seek is needed to protect public safety; for example, in an emergency, suspects can be asked where they hid their weapons.

19.   Maintenance of negative values and attitudes is believed to cause police officers to be secretive and isolated from the rest of society, producing what has been described by William Westly as the _____ _____ subculture.

20.   The law enforcement function of police is not merely a matter of enforcing the rule of law but also involves an enormous amount of personal _____ as to whether to invoke the power of arrest.

21.   In 1985, the Supreme Court moved to restrict police use of _____ _____ when in Tennessee v. Garner it banned the shooting of unarmed or nondangerous fleeing felons.

TRUE/FALSE

1.   Law enforcement in colonial America paralleled the German model.

2.   In colonial America, the justice of the peace became the most important law enforcement agent.

3.   The modern police department was born out of urban mob violence, which wracked the nation's cities in the nineteenth century.

4.   Police during the nineteenth century were generally incompetent, corrupt, and disliked by the people they served.

5.   The Boston police strike promoted police unionism for decades and solidified power in the hands of union leaders in their fight against a reactionary, autocratic police administration.

6.   Through the 1960s, police professionalism was interpreted as a tough, highly trained, rule-oriented law enforcement department organized along militaristic lines.

7.   Today's FBI is a police agency with jurisdiction over all matters in which the United States may be interested.

8.   The major role of state police today is controlling traffic on the highway system, helping trace stolen automobiles, and aiding in disturbances and crowd control.

9.   Most large urban police departments are agencies operating under specific administrative control of higher governmental authorities.

10.   The Police Foundation found that while foot patrols had little effect on improving citizen attitudes toward the police, they did help lower community crime rates.

11.   Research found that Operation Pressure Point successfully reduced drug trafficking in the area while at the same time it revived community spirit.

12.   The beat officer is the "backbone" of policing.

13.   Robert Sampson and Jacqueline Cohen found in their recent analysis of police activities in 71 Canadian cities with populations over 50,000 that departments which used a reactive, cool spot law enforcement system were less likely to lower burglary rates.

14.   In a classic study, James Q. Wilson and Barbara Boland found that police departments that use a proactive, aggressive law enforcement style may help reduce crime rates.

15.   Proactive police strategies are supported in minority areas where citizens believe they are more likely to be the target of residential burglaries.

16.   The most serious consequences of the police subculture are police officers' resistance to change and distrust of the public they serve.

17.   Police officers are regulated in their daily procedures by administrative scrutiny.

18.   When an officer chooses to become involved in a situation without benefit of a summons or complaint, maximum discretion can be used.

19.   Limiting police discretion has proved to be a relatively easy task.

20.   Because racial bias in arrest decisions violates constitutional rights, courts have prohibited the use of race as a personal identifying factor in helping narrow police searches for suspects.

21.   In United States v. Paradise, the Supreme Court upheld the use of racial quotas as a measure to counter the effects of past discrimination in police departments.

22.   Police departments around the nation began hiring females and assigning them patrol duties after the Illinois legislature passed a statute in 1893 requiring greater female involvement in policing.

152

23.	A variety of research studies shows that female officers are more likely to use deadly force than males because their smaller stature prevents them from using unarmed techniques to subdue suspects.

24.	The justification for the use of deadly force can be traced to English common law, in which almost every criminal offense merited a felony status and subsequent death penalty.

25.	David Greenberg found moderate evidence that police employment levels are positively related to crime-rate reductions.

26.	The Police Executive Research Forum found that if a crime is reported while in progress, there is a 33 percent chance of making an arrest; the arrest probability declines to 10 percent if the crime is reported one minute later, and to about 5 percent if 15 minutes have elapsed.

MULTIPLE CHOICE

1.	The police have been in the forefront of the public thought for most of the twentieth century because of:
	a.	urbanization
	b.	immigration from the South to the North
	c.	the growth of media
	d.	their use of weapons and arrest power
	e.	unionization

2.	The origin of U.S. police agencies can be traced back to early _____ society.
	a.	French
	b.	English
	c.	German
	d.	Spanish
	e.	Italian

3.	In 1326, the office of _____ was created to assist the shire reeve in controlling the county.
	a.	justice of the peace
	b.	watchman
	c.	constable
	d.	tithing
	e.	hundred

4.	The colonial sheriff:
	a.	engaged in patrol
	b.	sought out crime
	c.	reacted to citizens' complaints
	d.	was paid by the varimax system
	e.	none of the above ("a" thru "d")

5. _____ created the first formal U.S. police department in 1838.
   a. Washington, D.C.
   b. Mobile
   c. Chicago
   d. St. Louis
   e. Boston

6. The first technological breakthroughs in police operations came in the area of:
   a. transportation
   b. computers
   c. training
   d. communications
   e. firearms

7. The federal government maintains about _____ organizations that are involved in law enforcement duties.
   a. 10
   b. 30
   c. 50
   d. 75
   e. 100

8. A federal law enforcement agency under the direction of the Treasury Department:
   a. U.S. Marshals
   b. Immigration and Naturalization Service
   c. U.S. Border Patrol
   d. Alcohol, Tobacco, and Firearms Bureau

9. The current community policing "movement" was born when _____ _____ were reintroduced in a limited number of jurisdictions.
   a. team policing
   b. foot patrols
   c. motorized services
   d. ethical policing

10. A policing strategy aimed at reducing community fear levels:
    a. added value policing
    b. problem-oriented policing
    c. interactional patrols
    d. "fixing up" policing

11. Samuel Walker has criticized the broken windows concept on the grounds that:
    a. old style police were neither liked nor respected
    b. police have acted as crime busters during most of the twentieth century
    c. police enjoyed political acceptance during the nineteenth century
    d. police are quite capable of improving the community's perceptions of public safety
    e. all of the above ("a" thru "d") are criticisms

12. Police expert Jack Greene has found that in most community policing projects, the concept of "community" is defined in terms of:
    a. natural areas
    b. ecological areas
    c. ethnic areas
    d. racial areas
    e. administrative areas

13. Research findings on detective work suggest that:
    a. proactive efforts increase community perception that detectives arrest a lot of criminals
    b. aggressive detective strategies breed resentment among residents in core zones of urban areas
    c. a great deal of detectives' time was spent in productive work and that investigative expertise did much to help them solve cases
    d. when a suspect was identified, it usually occurred before the case was assigned to a detective
    e. detectives dropped 40 percent of cases after one week and spent an average of ten hours on each case

14. The _____ Amendment guarantees people the right to be free from self-incrimination.
    a. First
    b. Fourth
    c. Fifth
    d. Sixth
    e. Eighth

15. Which of the following is true about the Miranda rule today:
    a. initial errors by police in getting statements make subsequent statements inadmissible; a subsequent Miranda warning cannot "cure the condition" that made the initial statements inadmissible
    b. suspects must be aware of all the possible outcomes of waiving their rights in order for the Miranda warning to be properly given
    c. an attorney's request to see the suspect affects the validity of the suspect's waiver of the right to counsel; police misinformation to an attorney affects the waiver of Miranda rights
    d. the Miranda warning applies to attorneys, priests, and probation officers
    e. a person who is mentally ill due to clinically diagnosed schizophrenia may voluntarily confess and waive his or her Miranda rights

16. Threshold inquiry refers to:
    a. police informants
    b. aggressive reactive patrol tactics
    c. stop and frisk
    d. exams to ascertain the personality type of a police officer
    e. full enforcement vs. selective enforcement issue

17. A valid search may be conducted by police officers without a search warrant:
    a. when an object is in plain view
    b. in a stop and frisk situation
    c. when an automobile is searched
    d. none of the above ("a" thru "c")
    e. all of the above ("a" thru "c")

18.   Studies of policewomen show that:
   a.   arrests women made were more likely to result in conviction than men
   b.   women were less likely to receive support from the community than men
   c.   women were more likely to be charged with police misconduct than men
   d.   women made fewer felony and misdemeanor arrests than men
   e.   women received higher supervisory rating than men

19.   Research studies indicate that police violence is related to:
   a.   police workload
   b.   population type
   c.   exposure to stress
   d.   all of the above ("a" thru "c")
   e.   none of the above ("a" thru "c")

MATCHING

____	1.	Deadly force	A.	COINTELPRO
____	2.	Shire reeve	B.	Selective enforcement
____	3.	O.W. Wilson	C.	"Broken Windows"
____	4.	FBI	D.	"Double marginality"
____	5.	Secret Service	E.	Tennessee v. Garner
____	6.	Texas Rangers	F.	Quasi-military force
____	7.	Wilson and Kelling	G.	HITS
____	8.	Crack down	H.	Sheriff
____	9.	Traffic control	I.	Arm of the Treasury Department
____	10.	Valid search warrant	J.	Totality of the circumstances
____	11.	Technology	K.	Problem-oriented policing
____	12.	Black police officers	L.	Modern management techniques

---

ESSAY QUESTIONS

1.   Discuss the history of policing in England.

2.   How would you characterize American policing before the twentieth century?

3.   Discuss the development of professionalism in the twentieth century.

4.   What are the functions of the various law enforcement agencies on the federal level?

5.   Compare the duties of a county sheriff's department with metropolitan police agencies.

6.   Compare and contrast community policing with problem-oriented policing?

7.   Discuss community policing work? Explain.

8.   Define patrol. How effective is it?

9.   What are the roles of detectives? How effective are investigations?

10. Define custodial interrogation. What was the holding in the Supreme Court case of <u>Miranda v. Arizona</u> (1966)? How would you describe the status of <u>Miranda</u> today?

11. What was the ruling in the Supreme Court cases of <u>Illinois v. Gates</u>? Why is the ruling significant?

12. Under what circumstances can a valid search be conducted by police officers without a search warrant?

13. Describe the factors which influence the development of a police personality.

14. Identify and describe at least four factors that have been associated with the exercise of police discretion.

15. Discuss studies which focus on the influence of social factors on discretionary decision making.

16. What problems do female and black officers experience in police departments?

17. Discuss the findings of research studies that focus on factors related to police violence.

18. Describe efforts to control deadly force.

19. How has technology improved police effectiveness?

20. What are the problems with the expanded role of private security?

CHAPTER SIXTEEN ANSWER SECTION

FILL-IN REVIEW

1.	tithing		12.	aggressive
2.	constable		13.	internal affairs
3.	watch		14.	Kansas City
4.	Peel		15.	detective
5.	Wickersham		16.	sting
6.	Vollmer		17.	inevitable
7.	sheriff		18.	Miranda
8.	team		19.	blue curtain
9.	problem-oriented		20.	discretion
10.	Patrol		21.	deadly force
11.	beat			

TRUE/FALSE

1.	F	14.	T
2.	F	15.	F
3.	T	16.	T
4.	T	17.	F
5.	F	18.	T
6.	T	19.	F
7.	F	20.	F
8.	T	21.	T
9.	F	22.	F
10.	F	23.	F
11.	T	24.	T
12.	F	25.	F
13.	F	26.	T

MULTIPLE CHOICE

1.	d	11.	a
2.	b	12.	e
3.	a	13.	d
4.	c	14.	c
5.	e	15.	e
6.	d	16.	c
7.	c	17.	e
8.	d	18.	d
9.	b	19.	d
10.	b		

MATCHING

1.	E
2.	H
3.	L
4.	A
5.	I
6.	F
7.	C
8.	K
9.	B
10.	J
11.	G
12.	D

158

17 The Judicatory Process

LEARNING OBJECTIVES

1. Describe the state and federal court structures.

2. Describe the major responsibilities of the prosecutor, the defense attorney, and the judge.

3. Define prosecutorial discretion and the factors that influence its use.

4. Describe the problems with bail as well as efforts to reform bail.

5. Explain the benefits and liabilities of the plea bargaining process.

6. Identify and explain the major steps in the criminal trial from opening statements through sentencing and appeal.

7. Explain the scope of the following rights: to a speedy and public trial; to a jury trial; to be free from double jeopardy; to legal counsel; to competent legal representation; and to confront witnesses.

8. Identify and describe the four goals of sentencing.

9. Compare and contrast presumptive, structured, determinate, indeterminate, and mandatory sentencing.

10. Evaluate the effects of extralegal factors on sentencing outcomes.

11. Compare the arguments for and against the death penalty.

KEY TERMS AND CONCEPTS

U.S. district courts
Federal courts of appeal
U.S. supreme court
Writ of certiorari
Landmark decision
Affidavits
Public defenders
Adversarial process
Prosecutor
Prosecutorial discretion
Defense Attorney
Indigent defense systems
Judge
Missouri plan
Bill of indictment
Judicial overload
Bail

Bail bonding agent
Release on recognizance
Preventive detention
Plea bargaining
Diversion
Widening the net
Courtroom work group
Venire
Peremptory challenge
Direct examination
Cross examination
Speedy and public trial
Jury trial
Double jeopardy
Legal counsel
Competent legal
representation

Confront witnesses
Deterrence
Incapacitation
Rehabilitation
Desert/retribution
Concurrent sentence
Consecutive sentence
Indeterminate sentence
Determinate sentence
Sentencing guidelines
Structured sentencing
Mandatory sentencing
"Three strikes" laws
Sentencing disparity
Contextual discrimination
Death penalty

NAMES TO KNOW

Earl Warren	Edna Erez	Samuel Walker
Frank Miller	Pamela Tontodonato	Cassia Spohn
Wayne LaFave	Kenneth Culp Davis	Miriam Delone
Charles Breitel	Marvin Frankel	Thomas More
Louis Schweitzer	Michael Tonry	John Locke
Donald Newman	Marc Mauer	Immanuel Kant
Perry Mason	Stephen Klein	Michael Radelet
Roy Flemming	Joan Petersilia	Hugo Bedau
Peter Nardulli	Susan Turner	Charles Black
James Eisentein	Jimmy Williams	

FILL-IN REVIEW

1.   The U.S. _____ Courts are the trial courts of the federal court system.

2.   As the nation's highest appellate body, the U.S. _____ _____ is the court of last resort for all cases tried in the various federal and state courts.

3.   When the Supreme Court chooses to, it can word a decision so that it becomes a precedent that must be honored by all lower courts; this type of ruling is usually referred to as a _____ decision.

4.   The major role of the _____ is to represent the state in criminal matters that come before the court system.

5.   The _____ counsel performs many functions while representing the accused in the criminal process.

6.   Criminal defense attorneys are viewed as prime movers in what is essentially an _____ process: The prosecution and the defense engage in conflict over the facts of the case at hand, with the prosecutor arguing the case for the state and the defense counsel representing his or her client.

7.   The third major participant in the criminal trial is the _____--the senior officer in a court of criminal law.

8.   The judge formally _____ the jury by instructing its members on what points of law and evidence they must consider before reaching a decision of guilty or innocent.

9.   The defendant who is arraigned on an indictment or information can ordinarily plead guilty, not guilty, or _____ _____, which is equivalent to a guilty plea.

10.   _____ represents money or some other security provided to the court to ensure the appearance of the defendant at trial.

11.   When a defendant appears at trial, bail is returned and the _____ keeps the defendant's 10 percent.

160

12. The Federal Bail Reform Act of 1984 made release on _____ an assumption unless the need for greater control can be shown in court.

13. Rather than opposing each other in court, the prosecution and defense, sometimes aided by the magistrate, form a relationship that has been described as a courtroom _____ group.

14. The initial list of persons chosen in the jury selection process, which is called a _____, or jury array, provides the state with a group of potentially capable citizens able to serve on a jury.

15. Once the prospective jurors have been chosen, the process of _____ dire is begun; all persons selected are questioned by both the prosecutor and the defense attorney to determine their appropriateness to sit on the jury.

16. In addition to challenges for cause, both the prosecution and the defense are allowed _____ challenges, which let the attorneys excuse jurors for no particular reasons or for reasons that remain undisclosed.

17. If the defendant is convicted, the judge normally orders a presentence _____ by the probation department before imposing a sentence.

18. In a 1992 case, White v. Illinois, the Court again restricted the _____ clause by ruling that the state's attorney is neither required to produce victims in the child abuse cases nor demonstrate the reason they were unavailable to serve as witnesses.

19. If sentences are _____, they begin the same day and are completed when the longest term has been served.

TRUE/FALSE

1. Appeals from the district court are heard in one of the intermediate Federal Courts of Appeal.

2. The Supreme Court is composed of seven members appointed for 15 year terms by the president.

3. A government survey indicates that prosecutors in large counties are more likely to bring felons to trial than those in smaller, less crime-ridden counties.

4. The majority of criminal defendants are indigents who cannot afford legal counsel.

5. In general, the attorney list/assigned counsel system is used in most populated areas of the U.S.

6. In Nix v. Whiteside, the Supreme Court sustained an attorney's right to refuse to represent a client whom he suspected would commit perjury.

7. In most states, people appointed to the bench have a great deal of training in the role of judge.

8. The Sixth Amendment of the Constitution guarantees bail.

9. The deposit bail system is designed to replace the bail bondsman.

10. In the case of <u>Schall v. Martin</u>, the Supreme Court upheld a New York law providing for the preventive detention of a juvenile offender if the judicial authority believes the offender will be a danger to community safety.

11. Bail is one of the few areas in which people are seriously penalized because of their economic circumstances.

12. The plea bargaining process usually occurs between trial and sentencing.

13. When a defendant pleads guilty, it voids all prior constitutional errors made in that case.

14. Defendants who plead guilty are much more likely to be sent to prison than those who demand jury trials.

15. In most cases, the jury in a criminal trial consists of 8 persons, with 4 alternate jurors standing by to serve should one of the regular eight jurors be unable to complete the trial.

16. Normally, the defense attorney makes a closing statement first, followed by the prosecutor.

17. The verdict in a criminal case is usually required to be unanimous.

18. A defendant cannot waive the right to a speedy trial.

19. A person tried in federal court cannot later be tried in state court, and vice versa.

20. In the case of <u>Gideon v. Wainwright</u>, the Supreme Court granted the absolute right to counsel in all felony cases.

21. <u>Maryland v. Craig</u> signals that the Supreme Court is willing to compromise defendant's rights of confrontation in order to achieve a social objective, the prosecution of child abuse.

22. A single philosophy of justice holds sway when a sentencing decision is made.

23. The goal of desert involves prediction of behavior patterns.

24. The first prison sentences used in the United States were for a fixed period of years which the inmate was forced to serve before release.

25. Prescriptive sentencing guidelines are created by appointed sentencing commissions.

26. Considerable evidence is being assembled that the race and class of the victim and not the race and class of the offender may be the most important factor in sentencing decisions.

27. More than 200 of the inmates on death row today had prior homicide convictions.

28. People who kill whites are significantly more likely to be sentenced to death than people who kill blacks.

29. The Supreme Court has declared that mandatory death sentences are constitutional.

30. <u>McLesky vs. Kemp</u> may have been the last major challenge to the death penalty.

MULTIPLE CHOICE

1.   There are approximately _____ courts operating in the United States.
     a.   480
     b.   3,200
     c.   16,000
     d.   32,000

2.   When the U.S. Supreme Court decides to hear a case, it usually grants a writ of _____ requesting a transcript of the proceedings of the case for review.
     a.   <u>mandamus</u>
     b.   <u>prosequi</u>
     c.   <u>corpus</u>
     d.   <u>certiorari</u>

3.   U.S. attorneys are:
     a.   elected by the legislature
     b.   appointed by the Supreme Court
     c.   selected by the American Bar Association after recommendation by a governor's council
     d.   appointed by the president
     e.   selected by the Director of the Attorney General's Office in the Department of Justice

4.   Which of the following has been identified as influencing prosecutorial discretion:
     a.   plea bargaining
     b.   sentencing
     c.   conducting special investigations
     d.   office policy

5.   The Supreme Court has interpreted the _____ Amendment of the Constitution to mean that people facing trial for offenses that can be punished by incarceration have the right to legal counsel.
     a.   Eighth
     b.   Sixth
     c.   Fifth
     d.   Fourth
     e.   First

6.   Assigning private attorneys to represent indigent clients on a case-by-case basis is sometimes referred to as:
     a.   private defenders system
     b.   attorney list system
     c.   contract attorneys program
     d.   legal aid system

7.   About 16 states have adopted a three-part approach to select judges called the _____ Plan.
     a.   Neutral
     b.   Chicago
     c.   Alaska
     d.   Merit
     e.   Missouri

8. Under the U.S. system of justice, the right to bail comes from the _____ Amendment of the Constitution.
   a. Eighth
   b. Sixth
   c. Fifth
   d. Fourth
   e. First

9. Which of the following is <u>true</u> about plea bargaining:
   a. most courtroom participants support the abolition of plea bargaining
   b. the defendant is assumed to be not guilty in the pretrial settlement conference
   c. after plea bargaining was eliminated in Alaska, research found that the number of pleas changed significantly and prison sentences given to the most serious offenders increased
   d. the Supreme Court has ruled that a defendant's due process rights are not violated when a prosecutor threatens to reindict the accused on more serious charges if he or she does not plead guilty to the original offense
   e. none of the above ("a" thru "d") is true about plea bargaining

10. In a significant case, <u>Batson v. Kentucky</u>, the Supreme Court ruled that the use of _____ challenge to dismiss all black jurors was a violation of the defendant's right to equal protection of the law.
    a. causal
    b. discretionary
    c. peremptory
    d. venire
    e. contendere

11. The _____ Amendment to the Constitution provides for the right to a speedy and public trial by an impartial jury.
    a. Eighth
    b. Sixth
    c. Fifth
    d. Fourth
    e. First

12. At the close of the prosecutor's case, the defense actually asks the presiding judge to rule on a motion for a (an) _____ verdict.
    a. acquitted
    b. rebutted
    c. summated
    d. examined
    e. directed

13. The right to a speedy trial was made applicable by the Supreme Court to state courts through the Due Process Clause of the _____ Amendment in the case of <u>Klopfer v. North Carolina</u>.
    a. Twelfth
    b. Fourteenth
    c. Sixteenth
    d. Eighteenth
    e. Twentieth

14. Which of the following is <u>true</u> about jury trials:
    a. a jury trial is considered a fundamental right
    b. the Supreme Court held that defendants are entitled to a jury trial if they face the possibility of a prison sentence
    c. the Fifth Amendment specifies that a jury must have at least eight persons
    d. all of the above ("a" thru "c") are true
    e. none of the above ("a" thru "c") are true

15. The _____ Amendment provides that no person shall "be subject for the same offense to be twice put in jeopardy of life or limb."
    a. Eighth
    b. Sixth
    c. Fifth
    d. Fourth
    e. First

16. In the 1960s and 1970s, _____ became the prime goal of sentencing.
    a. deterrence
    b. incapacitation
    c. desert
    d. retribution
    e. rehabilitation

17. _____ is usually exacted for a minor crime and may also be combined with other sentencing alternatives.
    a. A fine
    b. A suspended sentence
    c. Probation
    d. A ticket
    e. Jail time

18. The basic purpose underlying the _____ sentencing approach, particularly during the middle of the twentieth century, has been to individualize each sentence in the interest of rehabilitating the offender.
    a. mandatory
    b. presumptive
    c. structured
    d. medical
    e. indeterminate

19. _____ sentencing generally limits the judge's discretionary power to impose any disposition but that authorized by the legislature; as a result, they reduce the idea of the individualized sentence.
    a. mandatory
    b. presumptive
    c. structured
    d. medical
    e. indeterminate

20. An extralegal factor which appears to influence sentencing is:
   a. seriousness of the offense
   b. offender's prior criminal record
   c. whether the offender used violence
   d. offender's economic status
   e. none of the above ("a" thru "d") is an extralegal factor

21. Which of the following is true about race.
   a. the greatest percentage of the African-American population lives in the South where prison sentences tend to be highest for all races
   b. after relevant legal factors were considered, race had little effect on sentencing outcomes in California
   c. the evidence seems to show that whereas racial and class discrimination may have been an important factor in the past, their direct influence on sentencing may be decreasing today
   d. there is evidence that blacks and poor whites are more likely to have prior records because of organizational and individual bias on the part of police
   e. all of the above ("a" thru "d") are research findings on sentencing outcomes

---

MATCHING

____	1.	Prosecutor	A.	Victim impact statement
____	2.	Case pressure	B.	Eighth Amendment
____	3.	Bill of indictment	C.	Release on recognizance
____	4.	Judicial selection	D.	People's attorney
____	5.	Bail	E.	Massachusetts Gun Control Law
____	6.	Vera Foundation	F.	Missouri Plan
____	7.	Diversion	G.	Rehabilitation
____	8.	Sentencing hearing	H.	Influences prosecutorial discretion
____	9.	Structured sentencing	I.	Death Penalty
____	10.	Mandatory sentencing	J.	Sentencing guidelines
____	11.	Gregg v. Georgia	K.	Widening the net
____	12.	Indeterminate sentencing	L.	Felony charge

ESSAY QUESTIONS

1. What are the similarities and differences between state judicial systems and the federal judicial system?

2. Explain the major duties of prosecutors.

3. What factors influence prosecutorial discretion?

4. Compare the three systems that have been developed to provide legal counsel to the indigent.

5. How do judges influence the operations of the local police and prosecutor's office?

6. What is the meaning and importance of the Missouri Plan to select judges?

7. What are the major problems with bail? Describe efforts to reform bail.

8.   What are the different plea bargaining arrangements that can be packaged in exchange for a guilty plea?

9.   What are the benefits of plea bargaining for the defendant as well as the prosecutor?

10.   What services are rendered by adult pretrial diversion programs?

11.   How are jurors selected?

12.   Discuss the basic steps in the criminal trial process.

13.   How speedy does a speedy trial have to be?

14.   Under what circumstances does an accused have a right to a jury trial?

15.   Discuss the four goals that are related to the imposition of a sentence.

16.   Explain the difference between concurrent and consecutive sentences.

17.   What are three variations on the indeterminate sentence?

18.   What extralegal factors have been linked to sentencing outcomes?

19.   What are the arguments for and against the death penalty?

20.   What have been some of the legal problems associated with the death penalty?

CHAPTER SEVENTEEN ANSWER SECTION

FILL-IN REVIEW

1.	District	11.	bondsman
2.	Supreme Court	12.	recognizance
3.	landmark	13.	work
4.	prosecution	14.	venire
5.	defense	15.	voir
6.	adversarial	16.	peremptory
7.	judge	17.	investigation
8.	charges	18.	confrontation
9.	nolo contendere	19.	concurrent
10.	Bail		

TRUE/FALSE

1.	T	16.	T
2.	F	17.	T
3.	F	18.	F
4.	T	19.	F
5.	F	20.	T
6.	T	21.	T
7.	F	22.	F
8.	F	23.	F
9.	T	24.	T
10.	T	25.	T
11.	T	26.	T
12.	F	27.	T
13.	T	28.	T
14.	F	29.	F
15.	F	30.	T

MULTIPLE CHOICE

1.	c	12	e
2.	d	13.	b
3.	d	14.	a
4.	d	15.	c
5.	b	16.	e
6.	b	17.	a
7.	e	18.	e
8.	a	19.	a
9.	d	20.	d
10.	c	21.	e
11.	b		

MATCHING

1.	D
2.	H
3.	L
4.	F
5.	B
6.	C
7.	K
8.	A
9.	J
10.	E
11.	I
12.	G

18 Corrections

LEARNING OBJECTIVES

1. Explain the various historical uses of punishment.

2. Describe correctional practices and reform in colonial America with comparisons between the Auburn and Pennsylvania systems of imprisonment.

3. Compare and contrast probation and parole.

4. Compare and contrast the uses of such intermediate sanctions as fines, forfeiture, restitution, shock probation, and split sentencing.

5. Define intensive probation supervision, house arrest, and residential community corrections. Explore the various programs implemented under each of these intermediate sanctions.

6. Describe the issues surrounding jails, and private prisons.

7. Differentiate among maximum, medium, and minimum security prisons.

8. Describe the different types of inmates and inmate cultures for male and female inmates.

9. Identify and describe the uses and usefulness of various correctional treatment programs.

10. List the major causes of prison violence and prison riots.

11. Identify and describe the major constitutional rights of inmates.

KEY TERMS AND CONCEPTS

Furtum manifestum
Capital and corporal punishment
Poor laws
Society for Alleviating the Miseries
    of Public Prisons
Walnut street prison
Penitentiary house
Auburn system
Pennsylvania system
Penologists
Probation
Intermediate sanctions
Day fines
Forfeiture
Monetary restitution
Community service restitution
Shock probation

Split sentencing
Intensive Probation Supervision
Diversion
Home Confinement
Surveillance Officers
Electronic monitoring
Residential community corrections
Jail and Prison
Minimum security
Medium security
Maximum security
maxi-maxi security
Private prisons
Total institution
Solitary confinement
Hustling
Inmate subculture

Inmate social code
Prisonization
Importation model
New inmate culture
La Familia
Aryan Brotherhood
Nuestra Familia
Surrogate family
Behavior therapy
Reality therapy
Transactional analysis
Milieu therapy
Work furlough
Free-venture programs
Hands-off doctrine
Parole
Parole grant hearing

NAMES TO KNOW

Henry VIII	Michael Agopian	John Irwin
Elizabeth I	Peter Jones	Donald Cressey
Marvin Wolfgang	Susan Turner	Charles Logan
William Penn	Terry Baumer	Paul Lerman
Benjamin Rush	Michael Maxfield	Robert Martinson
Alexis Durham III	Robert Mendelsohn	D.A. Andrews
Samuel Walker	Frank Cullen	Hans Toch
Z.R. Brockway	Bill McGriff	Charles Silberman
Thomas Mott Osborne	Gresham Sykes	Randy Martin
Joan Petersilia	Daniel Lockwood	Sherwood Zimmerman
Patrick Langan	James B. Jacobs	
Mark Cuniff	Donald Clemmer	

FILL-IN REVIEW

1. The _____ of criminals has undergone many noteworthy changes, reflecting custom, economic conditions, and religious and political ideals.

2. Poor _____ developed in the early seventeenth century required that the poor, vagrants, and vagabonds be put to work in public or private enterprise.

3. Although many people sentenced to death for trivial offenses were spared the gallows, there is little question that the use of _____ punishment rose significantly between 1750 and 1800.

4. In 1787, a group of Quakers led by Dr. Benjamin Rush formed the Philadelphia Society for Alleviating the _____ of Public Prisons.

5. At the _____ _____ Prison, most prisoners were placed in solitary cells, where they remained in isolation and had to earn the right to work through good behavior.

6. The philosophy of the _____ prison system was crime prevention through fear of punishment and silent confinement.

7. The warden at the Elmira Reformatory in New York, _____, advocated individualized treatment, the indeterminate sentence, and parole.

8. The alleged failure of correctional rehabilitation has prompted many _____ to reconsider the purpose of incapacitating criminals.

9. _____ and aftercare agencies supervise prisoners who have been given early release from their sentences.

10. Revocation for violation of probation rules is called a _____ violation; probation also can be revoked if the offender commits another offense.

11. _____ sanctions are a new form of corrections that fall somewhere between probation and incarceration.

12.   _____ can take the form of requiring convicted defendants to either pay back the victims of crime or serve the community to compensate for their criminal act.

13.   In a number of states and under the Federal Criminal Code, a jail term can actually be a condition of probation, known as _____ sentencing.

14.   _____ probation involves the resentencing of an offender after a short prison stay.

15.   The _____ is a secure institution used to (1) detain offenders before trial if they cannot afford or are not eligible for bail and (2) house misdemeanant offenders sentenced to terms of one year or less, as well as some nonserious felons.

16.   _____-security prisons, are surrounded by high walls and have elaborate security measures and armed guards.

17.   Part of inmates' early adjustment involves their becoming familiar with and perhaps participating in the hidden, black-market economy of the prison--the _____.

18.   One major aspect of the inmate subculture is a unique social _____--unwritten guidelines that express the values, attitudes, and types of behavior that the older inmates demand of younger inmates.

19.   Many prisons have adopted work _____ programs to allow inmates to work in the community during the day and return to the institution at night.

20.   Free _____ programs involve businesses set up by private entrepreneurs off prison grounds that contract with state officials to hire inmates at free-market wages and produce goods that are competitively marketed.

21.   In their oft cited research, _____ and his associates found that most treatment programs were failures. They found that rehabilitative efforts seemed to have no effect on recidivism.

22.   For many years, the nation's courts did not interfere in the operation of the prison, maintaining what is called the _____ doctrine.

23.   Some states with determinate sentencing statutes do not use parole boards but release inmates at the conclusion of their maximum terms less accumulated good time. This is _____ release.

TRUE/FALSE

1.   Misdemeanants are usually incarcerated in a county or state prison.

2.   The word <u>felony</u> comes from the twelfth century, when the term <u>felonia</u> referred to a breach of faith with one's feudal lord.

3.   Transportation to the colonies became very popular as a method of punishment at the same time as the colonial population increased, the land was further developed, and African slaves were imported in great numbers.

4. Opposition by organized labor helped put an end to the convict lease system and forced inmate labor.

5. The prison of the late nineteenth century was remarkably different from that of today.

6. By the mid-1930s, few prisons required inmates to wear the red-and-white-striped convict suit, most having replaced it with nondescript gray uniforms.

7. Community-based treatment is designed so that first time or nonserious offenders can avoid the stigma and pains of imprisonment and be rehabilitated in the community.

8. Probation implies a contract between the court and the offender in which the former promises to hold a prison term in abeyance while the latter promises to adhere to a set of rules or conditions required by the court.

9. It is common today for probation officers to participate in treatment supervision.

10. Day fines, a concept that originated in Europe, calibrates fines according to an offender's net daily income in an effort to make fines more equitable and fairly distributed.

11. Forfeiture is a new sanction.

12. Research indicates that those receiving restitution sentences have higher recidivism rates when compared to control groups of various kinds.

13. Two basic types of electronic monitoring systems are in use: active and passive.

14. Electronic monitoring is a labor intensive system rather than a capital intensive one.

15. Of the more than 500 adult prisons for men operating in this country, the overwhelming majority are federal institutions.

16. Medium-security facilities may employ dormitory living or have small private rooms for inmates.

17. In an important analysis by Charles Logan and Bill McGriff, privately run correctional institutions were found to provide better services at lower cost than public facilities.

18. Prisons may be the one institution in American society that blacks control.

19. Female inmates are often more likely than males to mutilate their own bodies and attempt suicide.

20. The most traditional type of treatment in prison involves vocational training.

21. Shock incarceration programs typically include youthful, first-time offenders and feature military discipline and physical training.

22. The costs of boot camp are lower than traditional prisons and since sentences are shorter boot camps do provide both short and long term savings.

23. Most studies conclude that a violence-overcrowding link exists.

24.   The hands-off doctrine was lifted in the 1980s.

25.   As a group, there is little evidence that alternative sanctions can prevent crime, reduce recidivism or work much better than traditional probation or prison.

MULTIPLE CHOICE

1.   In ancient times:
    a.   the most common state-administered punishment was whipping or capital punishment
    b.   execution of an offender was looked upon as the prerogative of the deceased's family
    c.   interpersonal violence which resulted in death was viewed as a harm to the whole community
    d.   all of the above ("a" thru "c") is true about punishment in ancient times

2.   During the last part of the eighteenth century, _____ types of crime in England were punishable by death.
    a.   70
    b.   350
    c.   700
    d.   3,500

3.   Correctional reform in the United States was first instituted in Pennsylvania under the leadership of:
    a.   Jeremy Bentham
    b.   Marvin Wolfgang
    c.   Z.R. Rockaway
    d.   William Penn

4.   The Auburn Prison design became known as the _____ system, because cells were built vertically on five floors of the structure.
    a.   level
    b.   structured
    c.   apartment
    d.   edifice
    e.   tier

5.   _____ was the key to prison discipline in the Auburn system.
    a.   Disablement
    b.   Training
    c.   Incapacitation
    d.   Intimation
    e.   Silence

6.   The Pennsylvania system:
    a.   was criticized for tempting inmates to talk by putting them together for meals and work and then punishing them when they did talk
    b.   eventually prevailed and spread throughout the United States
    c.   obviated the need for large numbers of guards or disciplinary measures
    d.   marched prisoners from place to place
    e.   none of the above ("a" thru "d") refers to the Pennsylvania system.

7. In post-civil war America, the congregate system was adopted in all states except
    _____.
    a. New York
    b. Massachusetts
    c. Connecticut
    d. Virginia
    e. Pennsylvania

8. Which of the following is a standard probation rule:
    a. maintaining steady employment
    b. making restitution for loss or damage
    c. meeting family responsibilities
    d. all of the above ("a" thru "c") are standard probation rules
    e. none of the above ("a" thru "c") are standard probation rules

9. Restitution:
    a. derived from the common-law concept of "corruption of blood" or "attaint"
    b. is used in conjunction with the RICO Act
    c. has been given a qualified success rating in most reviews
    d. all of the above ("a" thru "c") is true about restitution
    e. none of the above ("a" thru "c") is true about restitution

10. The primary goal of intensive probation supervision (IPS) is:
    a. restitution
    b. diversion
    c. rehabilitation
    d. desert
    e. deterrence

11. Which of the following is true about EM/HC programs:
    a. recidivism rates are higher than recorded for comparable groups of probationers or
        parolees
    b. adults responded better to these programs than juveniles
    c. they are the most secure intermediate sanction
    d. they have had little success with drunk drivers
    e. one evaluation found that the EM/HC works much more efficiently with convicted
        offenders than as a pretrial detention

12. This intermediate sanction program is considered more punitive than other community models and
    a "last chance" before prison:
    a. intensive probation supervision
    b. house arrest
    c. fines
    d. restitution

13. Which of the following is true about jails:
    a. the jail originated in eighteenth century colonial America
    b. on an annual basis, close to 10 million people are admitted to jail
    c. juveniles are prohibited from being housed in adult jails
    d. all of the above ("a" thru "c") are true about jails
    e. none of the above ("a" thru "c") are true about jails

14.   Today, there are more than _____ people in prisons.
        a.   330,000
        b.   580,000
        c.   830,000
        d.   1,100,000
        e.   1,350,000

15.   Clemmer defined _____ as the inmate's assimilation into the existing prison culture through acceptance of its language, sexual code, and norms of behavior.
        a.   acculturation
        b.   prisonization
        c.   institutionalization
        d.   absorption
        e.   chameleon

16.   In their <u>importation model</u>, Irwin and Cressey conclude that the inmate culture is affected by the values of _____.
        a.   newcomers
        b.   old timers
        c.   guards
        d.   convicts
        e.   peers

17.   Sociologist James B. Jacobs has found that:
        a.   the development of white racist power in the 1960s, spurred by the KKK, significantly influenced the nature of prison life
        b.   white inmates are much more cohesively organized than Latin inmates
        c.   only in California have white inmates failed in attempts at organizing themselves
        d.   all of the above ("a" thru "c") are findings of Jacobs' research
        e.   none of the above ("a" thru "c") are findings of Jacobs' research

18.   Women make up about _____ percent of the adult prison population.
        a.   one
        b.   five
        c.   nine
        d.   fourteen
        e.   eighteen

19.   A wide variety of innovative psychological treatment approaches have been used in the prison system. _____ therapy is meant to help satisfy individuals' needs to be worthwhile to themselves and others.
        a.   Milieu
        b.   Behavior
        c.   Transactional
        d.   Reality
        e.   Personal

20. Which of the following is an outcome of a court decision in the area of prisoners' rights:
    a. limited the right of an inmate to grant press interviews (Saxbe v. Washington Post)
    b. prohibited the practice of "double-bunking" (Rhodes v. Chapman)
    c. allowed the authorities to routinely censor an inmate's mail if any possibility exists that its contents would threaten morale in the prison (Procunier v. Martinez)
    d. all of the above are outcomes ("a" thru "c")
    e. none of the above are outcomes ("a" thru "c")

21. Which of the following is true about parole:
    a. parole is usually considered the same as a pardon
    b. parole is viewed as an act of grace on the part of the criminal justice system
    c. in most jurisdictions, the good time an offender accumulates cannot serve to reduce the minimum sentence
    d. very few parolees are returned to prison for technical violations
    e. the evaluation of parole effectiveness has produced positive results

MATCHING

1.	Parole prediction tables	A.	Maine and Indiana
2.	Auburn prison	B.	Electronic monitoring
3.	Pennsylvania prison	C.	Corrections Corporation of America
4.	Abolished parole	D.	Gagnon v. Scarpelli
5.	Probation revocation	E.	Salient Factor Score Index
6.	Rehabilitation	F.	Argot
7.	Forfeiture	G.	Zero tolerance
8.	House arrest	H.	"Total institution"
9.	RCC center	I.	Congregate system
10.	Private prisons	J.	"Nothing works" philosophy
11.	Prison	K.	"Halfway back"
12.	Unique language	L.	Reflected religious philosophy

ESSAY QUESTIONS

1. What were the limits of punishment during ancient and medieval times?

2. How were the poor laws used in the seventeenth and eighteenth centuries?

3. What were William Penn's contributions to corrections?

4. How did religious philosophy influence the Pennsylvania system?

5. What were the contributions of Z.R. Brockway to prisons?

6. Identify and describe the three trends that stand out during the modern era.

7. How is probation practiced in the United States?

8.   Identify five standard probation rules.

9.   How successful is probation?

10.   Is there a need for intermediate sanctions? Explain.

11.   Under what circumstances are fines and forfeitures used as sanctions?

12.   How well does restitution work?

13.   What is the primary goal of IPS? Who is eligible for IPS?

14.   Compare both active and passive electronic monitoring systems.

15.   Describe residential community corrections programs as "halfway in" and "halfway out" correctional approaches.

16.   What are the problems with the conditions in jails?

17.   What are the differences among maximum-security prisons, medium-security prisons, and minimum-security prisons?

18.   What are the potential problems with private prisons?

19.   Describe the personal characteristics of the typical prison inmate.

20.   What kinds of problems do males have in prisons?

21.   Define the "prisonization" process.

22.   What were the findings of Jacobs' research on the new inmate culture?

23.   Identify and describe two of the three basic types of roles in women's prisons.

24.   Identify and describe three types of therapy used in prison.

25.   Describe two of the three views on the causes of prison violence.

26.   What kinds of free speech and medical rights do inmates have?

27.   What factors influence parole board decision-making?

28.   How effective is parole?

29.   Describe two of the three criticisms that have been leveled against parole.

30.   What are the likely consequences of the abolition of parole?

CHAPTER EIGHTEEN ANSWER SECTION

FILL-IN REVIEW

1.	punishment		13.	split
2.	Laws		14.	shock
3.	capital		15.	jail
4.	Miseries		16.	maximum
5.	Walnut Street		17.	hustle
6.	Auburn		18.	code
7.	Brockway		19.	furlough
8.	penologists		20.	venture
9.	Parole		21.	Martinson
10.	technical		22.	hands-off
11.	alternative		23.	mandatory
12.	Restitution			

TRUE/FALSE

						MULTIPLE CHOICE			
1.	F	14.	F		1.	b	12.	b
2.	T	15.	F		2.	b	13.	b
3.	F	16.	F		3.	d	14.	c
4.	T	17.	T		4.	e	15.	b
5.	F	18.	T		5.	e	16.	a
6.	T	19.	T		6.	c	17.	e
7.	T	20.	F		7.	e	18.	b
8.	T	21.	T		8.	d	19.	d
9.	F	22.	F		9.	c	20.	a
10.	T	23.	T		10.	b	21.	b
11.	F	24.	F		11.	e		
12.	F	25.	T					
13.	T							

MATCHING

1.	E
2.	I
3.	L
4.	A
5.	D
6.	J
7.	G
8.	B
9.	K
10.	C
11.	H
12.	F